GOOD FOR ME!

GOOD FOR ME!

All About Food in 32 Bites

by Marilyn Burns/illustrated by Sandy Clifford

Little Brown and Company
Boston   Toronto   London

This Brown Paper School book was edited and prepared for publication at the Yolla Bolly Press, Covelo, California, in the winter and spring of 1978. The series is under the supervision of James and Carolyn Robertson. Production staff: Gene Floyd, Loren Fisher, Jay Stewart, Joyca Cunnan, and Diana Fairbanks.

First edition. Published simultaneously in Canada by Little, Brown & Company (Canada) Limited. Printed in the United States of America.

Library of Congress Cataloging in Publication Data

Burns, Marilyn.
    Good for me.

    (A brown paper school book)
    SUMMARY: An informative look at food and what it does for us.
    1. Food — Juvenile literature. 2. Nutrition — Juvenile literature. [1. Food. 2. Nutrition] I. Title.
TX355.B94   641.1   78-6727
ISBN 0-316-11749-8
ISBN 0-316-11747-1 pbk.

HC: 10 9 8 7 6 5   BP
PB: 15 14 13 12 11 10   BB

This book is for you, if you believe
that eating is more than just
exercise for your elbow.

What's in this book

1
Biting In

HEY, LOOK ... I'M AN EXPERT ON BITING AND LET ME TELL YOU I WOULDN'T BITE, LET ALONE SWALLOW, SOME OF THE THINGS YOU HUMANS DO! READ ON AND YOU MAY BECOME AN EXPERT TOO!

Eating. Now there's something you do every day, and it's one of the most important things you do every day too. Yet you probably don't know beans about that lunch you ate yesterday. About what it really did to you. And for you.

That's where this book comes in. This book is all about food — and you. It's about your body, what it likes to eat and needs to eat. It's about nutrition — practical nutrition that can help you keep your body in cheerful good health.

All through the book there's information about food. About why different foods taste different. How soda pop was invented and how hamburgers and potato chips came to be. About the lucky creation of the ice cream cone. About the daredevil feat when someone first ate a tomato. And what all these foods do for your body.

You'll learn about what the food experts think and what they don't all agree on. About what goes into breakfast cereals, hot dogs, and peanut butter. And about how all those foods get to the supermarket and to you.

There are activities for you to try, experiments to do, food quizzes to take — all designed to make you a food expert. After all, deciding what to eat is important. You make lots of those food decisions every day, and you'll be making those decisions for lots more years. This book aims to help you become your very own food expert.

WHY DO WE EAT WHAT WE DO?

BECAUSE IT LOOKS GOOD...

IT SMELLS GOOD...

IT TASTES GOOD...

IT'S NOT FATTENING...

IT IS FATTENING...

IT WILL MAKE ME STRONG...

IT'S GOOD FOR MY COMPLEXION...

IT'S WHAT MY BODY NEEDS...

I ALWAYS EAT WHEN I'M BORED

2
Your First Taste

First, here are some questions to give you a chance to see how much you know about the food in your life. Some of them, only you can answer. For others, the answers are given. Those answers are at the end of the questions. Go ahead and peek if you want. The idea is for you to get started becoming a food expert.

1. How many times a day, on the average, do Americans eat something? Not just meals but afternoon snacks, mid-morning munchies, nighttime nibbles.

2. How many times a day do you eat something?

3. What's in your refrigerator to eat right now?

4. Does your stomach ever "growl" or "talk"? Do you know why?

5. Do you know what foods you eat now that your parents didn't eat when they were your age?

6. Do you need to eat more than your mother does?

7. How many sections does an orange usually have?

8. How many jingles or slogans from food advertising can you think of?

9. Can someone be a vegetarian and still eat a healthy diet? Do you know what a vegetarian is?

10. What is "sugar crash"?

11. What kind of book outsells any other kinds? What does this have to do with food?

12. What's the use of food, anyway?

1. The average American has 20 food contacts every day. That means that Americans interrupt their day with something to eat or drink about 20 times. That's lots more than three square meals.

2. Keep tabs on yourself for two or three days. Carry a small index card in your pocket, and every time you eat something — a whole meal, a snack, a bite of a friend's apple, or a drink — count it as a food contact and mark it on your card.

3. You'll get plenty of chances to go and look as you read this book.

4. Most people's stomachs have something to say once in a while. You can find out why on page 35.

5. Ask them. Then check the chapter called "The Invention of Foods" for some more information about this.

6. Yes. Check page 26 to be sure.

7. Now how many years have you been eating oranges, and you never stopped to count? Try it next time. But take a guess first.

8. How many of those jingles or slogans were about vegetables? What do the jingles tell you about the nutritional value of the foods? You'll read more about food advertising all through this book.

9. Yes. Chapter 28 gives you the full scoop on that.

10. "Sugar crash" is something you can and should avoid. Chapter 9 has all that information.

11. Cookbooks. They were among the first kinds of books ever published, and they still outsell all other kinds. That shows how much people are really interested in food. There are some cookbooks written just for kids. Check the library or bookstore. You might even find one that makes your mouth water.

12. Ahhh, now you're ready to push on in this book. The next chapter begins to answer this one.

3
What's the Use of Food, Anyway?

Your body is the only one you get. It has to work for your entire lifetime, and it's equipped to do just that, but not without some help from you.

Your body, like an engine, needs fuel. That's where food comes in. You eat food, and the food you eat gives your body the fuel it needs. Your body needs that food to give you the energy to keep warm, walk, run, ride a bike, even move a finger. Your body also needs food to build and repair any parts needing service. And your body needs food to coordinate everything that goes on in it every day.

How does your body manage to do all this using the food you eat? Scientists have studied that process for quite some time. Here's what they've learned. Your entire body is made up of cells. Your muscles, bones, skin, blood, hair, everything is made up of tiny, tiny cells, so tiny that millions of them could fit inside a half-inch cube.

The cells that make up the different parts of your body have very different jobs to do. Your skeleton keeps you up, and the teams of cells that form it are concerned with your bones. Your heart keeps your blood moving. So the cells there have their work cut out for them. Teams of cells are busy throughout your entire body. Besides each team doing its own job, the teams have to coordinate with other teams in all parts of your body. That's because your heart and blood and skeleton and muscles and stomach and intestines and liver are all designed to serve the same body. Your body. It's a 24 hour a day job.

You are not the only thing made of cells. All of life on earth is, from small insects to enormous redwood trees. Without your cells, there wouldn't be much left of you. You'd be just a salty puddle of water that was full of chemicals and a few other things.

When you eat, you are providing the fuel for all of your cells. You are not just feeding one large life — you. When you eat, you are feeding trillions of very, very tiny lives.

That's some responsibility. The more you know about the food you choose to eat, the better you can serve every tiny cell in your body and serve yourself too.

4
What You Eat Matters

You and your cells don't really like the same foods. Cells aren't too crazy about chicken or hamburgers. They don't think too much of noodles or peanut butter either. At least not in the forms they're in when you eat them.

What your cells need for food are *nutrients*. Lucky for you, your body knows all about nutrients. Your body is a well-run chemical factory. You eat food and your body changes it to those nutrients the cells need and use for fuel. There are about 50 of these nutrients, and all of them are very important. Missing any one of them can lead to sickness and death.

There is no one food that supplies all of these nutrients. There was a time when people thought that as long as you ate enough food, you were doing just fine. Not so. You've got to eat the right combination of foods to make sure you're getting all the nutrients you need.

That's where *nutrition* comes in. Nutrition is the study of how food keeps you going. And it's only been during the past 200 years that people have been using science to sort out what's what nutritionally. That's not much time when you think that humans have been around and eating for hundreds of thousands of years or so.

What about those nutrients? How much do you know about how well you eat? Are you sure you're getting what you need?

It's easier to learn about the nutrients by organizing them a bit. They can be lumped into groups: carbohydrates, fats, proteins, vitamins, minerals, and water.

Nutritionists have studied which foods provide which nutrients and how much they provide. Then they've studied how much of each you need. Nutritionists agree that what they've learned is important for you to understand.

The Quickest Energy: Carbohydrates

Carbohydrates first. They're your main source of energy. Almost half of the foods most Americans eat every day are carbohydrates. Some foods that contain a good supply of carbohydrates are noodles, potatoes, bread, peas, beans, cereal, sugar, honey, and jam. Most of these foods are called sugars and starches, and most of them come from plant life. Do you regularly eat some of these foods?

When carbohydrates get into your body, they get changed into glucose. Glucose is just what your cells are waiting for. It does for cells what gasoline does for cars. It's the basic fuel. Glucose is actually a kind of sugar. When it gets into your cells, it burns. Not with a flame or with noise, but with a steady amount of heat. And that heat gives you energy.

Sometimes you may eat a lot of carbohydrates. When your body changes it to glucose, there's more fuel than your cells need right away. What then? Well there's always the chance that more fuel will be needed later, so your body can store the extra — or at least some of the extra.

This takes a bit of extra work for your body. There are some storage places in your body just for this purpose, but they aren't built to hold glucose. First your body has to change the glucose into another substance called glycogen. Then the glycogen can be stored, some in your liver, some in your muscles. Your body will store about a 12- to 48-hour reserve of extra glucose as glycogen. Then when you need some fuel, your body changes that glycogen back to glucose.

Sometimes there is still more glucose left over after your glycogen storage tanks are full. Your body changes that to fat, and your body can store lots of fat.

How come carbohydrates are called the quick energy? That's because when you eat a meal, the carbohydrates are first out of your stomach and on the way to providing energy for your body. Did you ever hear people joke about eating Chinese food and being hungry an hour or so later? There's some truth to that. Chinese food in restaurants is often high in carbohydrates: rice, noodles, bean sprouts, bamboo shoots. Since carbohydrates are first through the stomach, someone could feel a bit empty a few hours after eating them.

16

Facts About Fats

Fats are another group of nutrients and are also a good source of energy. Fats are found in lots of different foods. The fat on a piece of meat is a solid example. Oils are fats in liquid form.

Some of the fats you eat are invisible. They're in foods, but you don't see them, like the butterfat in milk, or the fat that's in eggs, meat, nuts, and cheese.

In a piece of meat, like a steak, even if you trimmed off all the fat you could see, about 10 percent of the meat itself would still be fat.

Then there are the visible fats. You may not see them all yourself, but whoever cooks the foods you eat sees the fat because they put it in — like the butter your eggs get scrambled in, the shortening used to cook French fried potatoes, or the oil put into the salad dressing.

You can store almost an unlimited amount of fat in your body. This is done under every part of your skin, between the muscles, around many of your organs, and even in the hollows of your bones. It's stored as an energy reserve of heat and fuel. When your body starts to need more fuel than you've provided by eating, and your glycogen storage tanks are empty, it will start to convert the fat you've stored back into fuel.

When you eat, fats are the slowest of all foods to be digested. They can stay in your stomach for up to four and a half hours before being pushed on.

Fats provide fuel differently than carbohydrates do. Fats burn more slowly. Think about cooking on a barbeque and using charcoal for fuel. When it's time for the charcoal to be lit, people usually use some kind of fast-burning starter fluid. That way the charcoal catches fire easily. The charcoal burns for a long time, slowly and evenly. It doesn't burn out soon like the starter does. It's the same kind of thing with carbohydrates and fats. The carbohydrates are the fast energy provider. Fats give a steady, slow-burning fuel to your cells. You need both of them.

Proteins: The Stuff of Life

No plant or animal can live without proteins. Every type of cell in all living things contains its own kinds of proteins. That's why proteins are very, very important. This is one of those groups of nutrients that your body absolutely must have.

Proteins make up about three-fourths of all the solid matter in your body, including your hair, muscles, bones, brain, fingernails, glands, teeth, and on and on. Each of these parts has its own special job, and each protein needed is custom made to both build and repair these parts.

You can't build muscles without protein. But protein alone isn't enough. Protein will help develop muscles and keep them healthy, but it's up to you to build up their strength. That takes exercise.

Proteins are the most complicated substances that people know about. There are millions of different proteins. All of them are put together from what are called amino acids. But there aren't millions of amino acids. There are only 20 or so of them.

Now how can only 20 amino acids make millions of proteins? Just like you spell words with the 26 letters of the alphabet. Proteins are made by linking together different assortments of amino acids. Not every amino acid is used in every protein, and some are used more than once in some proteins.

There are proteins in most of the foods you eat, but some foods contain a larger percentage of protein than others, like eggs, meat, fish, poultry, nuts, and milk. Nutritionists have found that just eating a lot of proteins is not enough. Those 20 amino acids are crucial to your health.

Your body needs all of those amino acids. Some of them, your body can manufacture itself. Remember, your body is a terrific chemical plant. But there are 8 of those amino acids that your body cannot manufacture, and it is absolutely essential that you have them. In fact, these 8 are called the *essential amino acids*, even though all 20 are really necessary. So though many foods may provide proteins, not all foods provide the kinds of proteins that have those 8 special amino acids.

In general, animal proteins contain all the essential amino acids, so they are called *complete* proteins. Vegetable proteins are often *incomplete*. Some foods that do give your body complete proteins are meat, milk, poultry, eggs, fish, soybeans, cheese. Other foods with a useful amount of protein are nuts, potatoes, dried beans, whole wheat bread, whole grain rice and cereals. It's possible to combine two of these incomplete proteins to make complete proteins that supply all you need. When you add milk to dry breakfast cereal, for example, you are completing the protein in the cereal.

Even though the protein you eat is so important, it isn't what you eat most of. An adult eats about 1,000 pounds of food in a year. Only about 100 pounds of that food is protein. How much protein you need depends on how much you weigh. Nutritionists don't all agree here, but one formula that seems most generally used is that if you take your weight in pounds and multiply it by .424, the result will tell you how many grams of protein you should eat each day. Around 44 grams is the amount usually given for kids, 11 to 14 years old.

But unless you know what makes up 44 grams of protein, that information isn't much use to you. Here are some examples of how much complete protein you get from some foods:

1 EGG 6 GRAMS

1 GLASS OF MILK 9 GRAMS

1 HAMBURGER (TWICE THE SIZE OF A McDONALD'S REGULAR) 21 GRAMS

1 CHICKEN DRUMSTICK 12 GRAMS

1 HOT DOG 7 GRAMS

1 SCOOP OF ICE CREAM 2 GRAMS

1 PORK CHOP 15 GRAMS

Do you need extra protein if you're going to be doing something extra hard? No, it wouldn't do you any extra good. If you eat more protein than your body needs, the extra just gets changed into glucose. Then it's either used for fuel, changed to glycogen, or stored as fat.

19

The Vitamin Story

You need your vitamins. You've probably heard that before, and it's true. Not only do you need them, you've got to be sure to get them from somewhere, because your body can't manufacture them for you. In that way, they're like the essential amino acids.

About 100 years ago, a biochemist, Nikolai Lunin, reported on some experiments he did with mice. He took two groups of mice and did a nutritional investigation. He fed one group food in a concentrated form that had all the nutrients that were known then. Those mice got sick and died in a few weeks. The other group of mice got fed only milk, and they lived. He decided that milk probably had some substances that were absolutely necessary for good nutrition.

This theory of his was ignored. But in the early 1900s other scientists began to discover and consider these "other substances." In 1911 a Polish chemist, Casimir Funk, named them. Since then, scientists have continued their study and have learned more about these substances, which are the vitamins you need to live.

There are 13 vitamins known today that your body needs: A, C, D, E, K, and the eight parts of the vitamin B group. These vitamins are all found in food; another reason why it's important to eat a balanced diet.

THE VITAMIN FAMILY

Some people take vitamin pills to make sure they're getting what they need. Some nutritionists say this is a good idea. Other nutritionists say nonsense, you get what you need from food and you don't need extras. Some say that too many vitamins can be harmful. It's a difficult subject to sort out, and people feel very strongly about what they believe. Check the chapter on vitamins for some more specific information about vitamins and this nutritional quarrel.

Still, all nutritionists agree on one thing. You do need your vitamins.

Minerals, Too

Your body needs about 20 known minerals. They make up another nutrient group. These minerals are found in food in tiny amounts.

Eight of those minerals are calcium, chloride, iron, magnesium, phosphorus, potassium, sodium, and sulfur. These are the ones you need the largest amounts of, but still the amounts you need of them are very small, from 1/30 to 1/30,000 of an ounce per day. Even though that's not much, you do need your daily allotment.

HAVE YOU HAD YOUR MINERALS TODAY?

Of these eight minerals, nutritionists have found that the only ones that are sometimes lacking in people's diets are calcium and iron.

Calcium is needed mainly for your skeleton, with a little bit needed for your teeth. Three glasses of milk each day gives you the calcium you need. You can also get the calcium you need from yogurt, cheese, broccoli, baked beans, and dark green leafy vegetables.

Iron is a necessary part of your blood. Liver is the best source of iron, but you can get iron from red meats, nuts, eggs, seafoods, prunes, raisins, and whole grain breads and cereals.

The other nine minerals are called trace elements. You only need a few millionths of an ounce per day of each of these. Not much for stuff with such fancy names — chromium, cobalt, copper, flouride, iodine, manganese, molybdenum, selenium, and zinc.

Only one of these nine makes nutritionists nervous — iodine. That's why iodine has been added to table salt. Check the box of salt in your house or check one in a market. If it's labeled "iodized," then it has iodine added. Without enough iodine, people get a disease called *goiter*. Goiter affects the thyroid gland, which is in your neck. Up until the early 1900s, it was quite a problem in certain states in the United States: Washington, Oregon, Montana, Idaho, Utah, Wyoming, Wisconsin, and Michigan, as well as in others.

Your Watery Body

Water is more than a thrist quencher. It's another important nutrient that your body cannot do without. You could live for several weeks without food, though it's not a good idea to try it, but you could live barely one week without water.

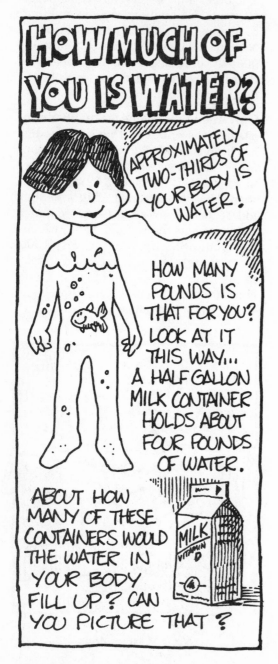

The water in your body is in your blood, all around your cells, and in your cells too. Water carries nutrients to all your cells and carries wastes from the cells. It does this through your bloodstream.

When you are thirsty, your body needs more water. If it's real hot out or if you exercise hard and sweat a lot, you get thirsty often. That's because you lose water from your body when you sweat, and so your body gives you the signal to drink some more.

There's water in all the foods you eat. Some foods contain more, some less. A glass of milk is 87 percent water. A hamburger is a little more than half water. Celery is 94 percent water; a raw carrot, 88 percent; a baked potato, 75 percent. A slice of bread is 36 percent, unless you toast it; then it goes down to 25 percent. Even corn flakes have a little bit of water in them, only 4 percent though.

There's One More Essential

There's one more thing you cannot live without, and you don't have to eat to get it. All you have to do is breathe. It's oxygen.

Some nutritionists include oxygen as one of the essential nutrients. Others don't call it a nutrient because you don't get your oxygen supply from food. But either way, it doesn't really matter. As long as you get your supply, your body will be satisfied.

Without oxygen, there would be no way for your body to burn the food it uses as fuel. There really is a tiny fire burning inside each cell in your body — not with flames or smoke but giving off steady, gentle heat. All your cells giving off this heat together keep you warm.

Fuel and oxygen are needed to keep anything burning. A birthday candle, for instance, burns by using the wax for fuel and combining that fuel with oxygen.

TRY PUTTING A JAR OVER A CANDLE...

...AND SEE HOW QUICKLY...

...IT GOES OUT!

Take a hamburger, for example. It's a good supplier of protein, so it's sometimes called a protein food. But only 20 to 25 percent of its weight is protein. The rest is fat, various vitamins and minerals, and water.

A glass of milk gives you 9 grams of complete protein, but it also provides some fat and carbohydrate value, as well as being rich in vitamins.

French fried potatoes provide more carbohydrates than any other nutrient, but they also provide some protein, some fat, vitamins and minerals too. A raw carrot will provide some carbohydrate, less protein, and hardly any fats but will give you enough vitamin A for your daily need.

There's one exception to the rule that foods give you an assortment of nutrients. That exception is the sugar found on most American kitchen tables. Sugar is pure carbohydrate. It offers no other nutritional value whatsoever. You do need carbohydrates, that's for sure. But it's important not to overdo the sugar and then not have room for what else your body needs. You could even live without adding any sugar to your foods at all, if you could convince your sweet tooth.

When you play hard, all those fires in your cells burn faster, so you get hotter. Then your breathe harder. That's because the cell fires are using up more oxygen and you need more.

Without oxygen, you couldn't live very long. Maybe five minutes, no more. It's very, very important.

Where the Nutrients Are

Even though some foods are listed as good sources for protein, or carbohydrates, or calcium, most foods offer a combination of nutrients.

LIVE WITHOUT SUGAR? I'D DIE!

5
How Much You Eat Matters

How much food do you need to eat? Just enough to keep you from being hungry. That's a quick answer and not a bad one. Your appetite is your body's signal for when you're hungry or have had enough. If you eat well when you're really hungry, you'll probably do okay.

GETTING THE PICTURE...

Here's a way to get a picture of how much you eat. Make a list of everything you eat in a day. One way to do this is to make a chart like this and carry it with you for a day.

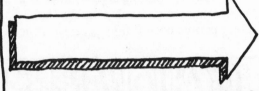

When you've got your chart completed for one day, you get to start your picture. Collect some old magazines, the kind of home magazines that usually have food ads in them. Search through and cut out pictures of what's on your list. What you can't find, draw on a piece of paper and cut out. Or you can actually take the label from a candy bar or can of soup. Arrange the whole collection on a piece of stiff paper or cardboard and glue it down. Some picture, huh?

	FOOD	ABOUT HOW MUCH
BREAKFAST		
MID MORNING		
LUNCH		
AFTERNOON		
DINNER		
AFTER DINNER		

Nutritionists have studied this question — how much food you need to eat — very carefully. They know you get energy from the food you eat, and you burn up energy all day, whether you're sleeping, walking, or running down the street. The amount of energy you get from food should equal the amount of energy you use up. Simple enough? Only if you know how to measure all that energy.

Energy can be measured. When you measure how much you weigh, you use pounds or maybe kilograms. If you measure how tall you are, you use inches or centimeters. When you measure energy, you use a unit of measurement called a Calorie.

What's a Calorie?

Energy is measured by calculating the amount of heat produced when food is burned. A calorie is a unit of measurement used to describe that heat. A Calorie is the amount of heat needed to raise the temperature of a kilogram of water, which is a little more than a quart, one degree centigrade. It's important to write Calorie with a capital C. A calorie with a small c is a unit of heat also, but only 1/1000 of a Calorie.

A glass of whole milk gives 160 Calories of energy. A slice of whole wheat bread gives 65 Calories. An apple gives 70 Calories. A chicken drumstick gives about 90 Calories.

You need to know how much energy you spend in a day to know how many Calories of food you need to eat. There is an official government estimate of how many Calories you need daily. It's called the Recommended Daily Allowance, abbreviated RDA. It's been figured out by experts in nutrition. Use this chart to find how many Calories you need to eat in a day, and see how much everyone else in your family needs too.

Compare how many Calories you need to supply your daily energy needs with how many your mother and father each need. Then compare your size with your mother's and father's sizes. You're probably smaller than they are, yet you may need even more daily Calories than one or both of them. Kids burn fuel faster than grownups. You're still growing and your body is building all the time. That's why you need as much or more than older people even though you weigh less.

RECOMMENDED DAILY ALLOWANCES

	AGE	WEIGHT (POUNDS)	HEIGHT (INCHES)	ENERGY (CALORIES)
CHILDREN	1-3	28	34	1300
	4-6	44	44	1800
	7-10	66	54	2400
MALES	11-14	97	63	2800
	15-18	134	69	3000
	19-22	147	69	3000
	23-50	154	69	2700
	51+	154	69	2400
FEMALES	11-14	97	62	2400
	15-18	119	65	2100
	19-22	128	65	2100
	23-50	128	65	2000
	51+	128	65	1800

"Aha," you might say, "I've got lots of Calories to eat every day. Potato chips, candy, soda won't hurt. I need my Calories, you know." Careful there. There's a snag or two in that thinking. There is a danger that you'll fill up on all that first before making sure you're getting what your body really needs. Those nutrients, remember. You've heard "don't eat before dinner, you'll spoil your appetite." There's something to that.

The figures on the chart are averages. Every body is different. Some people are more active than others. Some people weigh less than others. So take the information as a general guideline, not as an absolute rule. And if you spend a whole day riding your bike on a long trip, you'll spend more energy than if you curl up on a rainy day with a book.

EVERYBODY IS DIFFERENT... AND OUR BODIES HAVE DIFFERENT NEEDS...

The Calories in Food

Now that you know about how many Calories you need each day, how can you find out how many Calories you get from the food you eat? In a nutrition lab, that would be easy.

Suppose you want to find out the food energy in a slice of bread. You need to burn the bread and see what it does to the temperature of a kilogram of water. This can be done in a special instrument called a calorimeter. That's a closed box with a kilogram of water in it, a way to burn the food, and a thermometer to read the temperature.

Lucky for you, and for anyone else who is interested, that's all been done for you. Nutrition experts have worked out the Calories in all sorts of food. You'll find that information on most cans, jars, and packages of food. Check a can in your kitchen cupboard to see if you can find the Calories for an average serving.

Just to give you an idea, here are some foods that will give you close to 100 Calories.

1 large apple
1 medium banana
1 small hamburger (not the bun, just the meat)
2 thin slices of whole wheat bread
2 pats of butter
9 potato chips
1 cup of orange juice
1 brownie
2 chocolate chip cookies
10 medium dill pickles
1 tablespoon of peanut butter
2 tablespoons of sugar
8 ounces of cola
1 large ear of corn
1 scrambled egg
20-25 peanuts
1 cup of corn flakes

There Is a Catch

Remember, Calories aren't everything. Check back in Chapter 4 if you need reminding about the nutrients your body needs.

Suppose you decided that all you wanted for breakfast was a big piece of chocolate cake with chocolate icing and a can of cola to wash it down. That would give you a total of 380 Calories. Or suppose you decided to have a piece of toast with butter, a scrambled egg, and a glass of milk. That would give you not quite as many Calories — only 370.

If you're interested in more specific information about the Calories in different foods and the amount of protein, fat, carbohydrates, and other nutrients, you can get that information in different ways. You can check with the librarian and ask for a chart of the nutritional values of foods. Or you can write for the booklet *Nutritive Value of Foods* from the U. S. Government Printing Office, Washington, D. C. 20402. Then you can tell how many Calories there are in just about everything you eat.

But check the differences on the chart. And think about how your body would like those choices for breakfast.

	CALORIES	PROTEIN (GRAMS)	FAT (GRAMS)	CARBOHYDRATES (GRAMS)
CHOCOLATE CAKE	235	3	9	40
CAN OF COLA	145	0	0	37
TOTALS	380	3	9	77
TOAST WITH BUTTER	100	3	5	14
A SCRAMBLED EGG	110	7	8	1
A GLASS OF MILK	160	9	9	12
TOTALS	370	19	22	27

How Much Did
Diamond Jim Stomach?

Diamond Jim Brady didn't worry about Calories. He had an appetite you will need all your imagination to believe.

First of all, he was an orange juice nut. He drank a gallon of orange juice at breakfast. That helped to wash down what he usually ate — the eggs, cornbread, hominy, muffins, flapjacks, chops, fried potatoes, and steak.

He had a snack just before noon. He ate lunch at 12:30. That meal was usually made up of oysters or clams, two or three deviled crabs, broiled lobster, some beef, salad, and several kinds of pies. And some more orange juice, of course.

He liked to have a platter of food with afternoon tea.

Dinner was more oysters, more crabs, at least two bowls of soup, six or seven lobsters, duck, a steak, vegetables, dessert, all with some lemon soda to drink. And more orange juice. He'd finish off dinner with a box of candy. That held him until his late evening snack, usually a couple of roasted fowl and some bottles of lemon soda.

When he was 56 years old, his stomach rebelled. He became seriously ill and died five years later, in 1917. His stomach was six times as large as a normal person's.

6
Once You Swallow

Do you know what actually happens to the food you eat once you swallow it? It's a pretty fascinating story.

You'll eat an enormous amount in your lifetime. Not as much as Diamond Jim, hopefully, but enough to allow 23,000 pounds of solid food and 45,000 quarts of fluid to pass through your mouth. That amounts to about half a ton each year.

It's up to you to get the food into your body. You're the one who lifts the food to your mouth, puts it in, and chews it.

But once you swallow, it's a different story. Your body takes over automatically and gets right into action.

Your body is actually a chemical factory, a very fancy, walking chemical factory. Your body breaks down and changes food you swallow into substances your cells need for fuel and building. All you've got to do is eat a meal, or even a snack, and your body gets to work. It continues to work on that food for maybe as long as twelve hours too. The work is called *digestion* and here's what happens.

The First Signal

Your body gets started working even before you swallow. When you put food into your mouth, your body gets the first signal. A message gets sent right to the brain: Hey, here comes some food again. Then an order gets sent to certain glands, your salivary glands. They produce saliva in your mouth. That's so as you chew, the food begins to soften. The saliva also gets the whole chemical action of digestion started.

Your salivary glands will send saliva into your mouth without you eating something. Your brain will send the signal for saliva even if you just see or smell food or even when you think of something that is real tasty.

THE MAKE-YOUR-OWN-SALIVA TEST

TRY IT... THINK OF SOMETHING THAT IS ABSOLUTELY DELICIOUS TO EAT — YOUR FAVORITE SNACK. CLOSE YOUR EYES AND IMAGINE TAKING A TASTE. IMAGINE HOW GOOD IT IS. NOW FEEL THE AMOUNT OF SALIVA IN YOUR MOUTH. GOOD TRICK, SENDING THAT SIGNAL TO YOUR BRAIN AND MAKING YOUR MOUTH WATER!

Food isn't all you take in through your mouth. You can take air in too. Breathing through your mouth can be handy, especially when you have a bad cold. The air you breathe in goes into your lungs, but the food is headed for your stomach. At the back of your throat there's an intersection with two choices. The windpipe is one choice; it goes to your lungs. The other is the esophagus. That's the pipe that goes to your stomach. When you swallow, a trap door slams shut, covering your windpipe and sending the food on its way to your stomach.

You can feel how your trap door works. Breathe through your mouth a few times. When you've got that going, swallow. What happened to your breathing? No more air could go down the windpipe. The trap door shut. If you do happen to swallow some air and send it down to your stomach, you may belch it up. Babies burp after they eat because they usually swallow some air with their food.

The Trip Down

It's a quick trip down your esophagus to your stomach, about one second for liquids and six to seven seconds for solid food. But the food doesn't just drop down, pulled by gravity. It gets sent along by muscles which stretch the length of your esophagus and force the food down. The way the muscles do this is like toothpaste being squeezed along in a tube, so the trip happens even if you're standing on your head when you swallow. That's why astronauts can eat even when there's no gravity to pull on their bodies.

Chickens' bodies don't have this. When they take something in their mouths, they have to tilt their heads back so it can slide down. But horses and cows graze with their heads down; they have no trouble getting the food into their stomachs.

31

Meantime, while the food starts down your esophagus, your stomach gets the message that food is on its way. That message is a signal to start releasing the chemicals the stomach needs to do its part of the digestion job.

The Big Masher: Your Stomach

When your stomach gets the food you've swallowed, it gets to work on it. It mashes it. It churns it. It pulverizes it. Soon it's battered beyond recognition of what you ate, and a good thing, too, because that's how food starts to become fuel for your body.

Do you know where your stomach is? It's not around your navel. It's higher up than that and over to the left. There it sits, all glossy and pink on the outside and shiny velvety on the inside.

When your stomach is empty, it's like a deflated balloon. When you eat, it begins to fill up and can hold almost two quarts when full. Think about two-quart containers of milk to give you an idea of how much that is. Eat more than that and you'll feel it. You may know that stuffed feeling from having pigged it up sometime.

Your stomach works on the food you eat like a cook kneading bread, and while it's mushing, it's adding digestive juice that helps to break the food down.

That juice contains hydrochloric acid, a powerful acid. It can be used to dissolve cement. You wouldn't want to touch it with your fingertip; it would eat your skin right away. But your stomach finds it very useful in breaking down that food and changing it into a yellowish mash called *chyme*. Sometimes when you burp, it's caused by that acid, not because you swallowed some air.

THE ACID TEST

WHEN SODA POP HITS YOUR STOMACH, THERE'S A QUICK REACTION. YOU CAN SEE WHAT THIS IS LIKE. PUT SOME SODA POP IN A GLASS AND ADD A FEW DROPS OF VINEGAR.

IMAGINE THAT HAPPENING IN YOUR STOMACH. IT DOES HAPPEN A LITTLE BIT WITH EVERY MEAL YOU EAT.

Your stomach has a protective lining inside that is a layer of mucus. That's so the hydrochloric acid doesn't attack your stomach along with the food and digest it too. Your stomach is a tough pouch. When you get a scratch on your skin, how long does it usually take for it to heal and all traces of it to disappear? Five days? A week maybe? Well, if your stomach gets a scratch, say from a piece of fishbone, it will heal completely in 24 hours.

Your stomach takes its time doing its job. It holds on to a meal you eat for as long as four and a half hours. That's why you don't have to eat every half hour, though sometimes you may feel like you want to.

All of the time the food is in your stomach, it's being worked down toward a valve at the bottom of your stomach. This valve is called the *pylorus*.

The Small Intestine
Isn't Small at All

The small intestine starts right on the other side of the pylorus. Your stomach pushes that yellowish gruel through the pylorus, but not all at once. It does it in little squirts, about one every 20 seconds. That's how the food enters your small intestine.

The small intestine is a tube about an inch and a half in diameter, coiled in your body like a pile of rope. Uncoiled it's more than 20 feet long. It's where most of the chemical digestion of your food takes place. The small intestine pushes those little squirts from your stomach along by that toothpaste-tube method, mixing it with more digestive juices.

Part of the job of your small intestine is to separate what your body can use from what isn't useful and will be discarded as waste. It's got a filter system that helps with that. The inside of your small intestine is lined with millions of tiny, soft, hairlike projections, each about the size of a comma on this page. They're called *villi*. All together, these villi make a kind of shaggy carpet. All of the villi have tiny blood vessels in them. As the food gets pushed along in your small intestine, the villi take what your body can use into your blood stream by absorbing it through blood vessels. Some of this goes directly to your liver, the rest goes to other parts of your body.

It takes anywhere from three to eight hours to get a meal entirely through your small intestine.

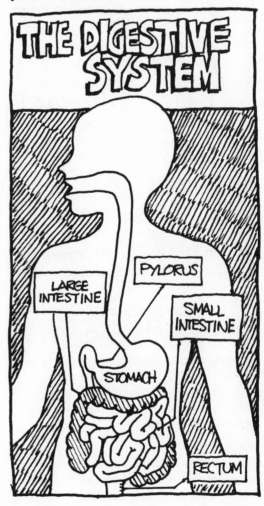

33

The Large Intestine, Which Isn't So Large

What the body can't use gets pushed all the way to the end of the small intestine and into the large intestine. Your large intestine is only five feet long, but it's a fatter tube than your small intestine, maybe two and a half inches in diameter. It's curled around the pile of your small intestine like an upside-down U. What goes into the large intestine stays there for 10 to 12 hours. During that time, most of the water gets absorbed out, leaving the solid waste that is expelled through your rectum when you have a bowel movement.

The Virtuoso Liver

The liver is truly amazing. It's the most complicated organ in your body. It produces over 1,000 chemicals and does 500 or so jobs. A chemical company would need an enormous factory to do what the liver does.

Before the food you eat gets to your liver, it's been broken down in your stomach and small intestine into substances the body can use. What the liv-

er does is just the opposite. It recombines those substances into the special mixtures needed by the different parts of the body and sends them out to where they're needed. It's a kind of made-to-order-and-delivery operation.

Here are just a few of your liver's talents. When you cut yourself, the liver will produce just the substance that's needed to clot your blood so it doesn't keep spilling out. As the body needs fuel, the liver reconverts the excess it has stored and releases it. Cells throughout your body are continually regenerating. The liver sends out what is needed to do this and does this service for all the parts of your body. Take your red blood cells, for example: millions of them die each second. The liver salvages what is possible to use to build new ones. The liver can rebuild itself, too, if part of it is damaged; though a damaged liver is a serious problem and it's best to take good care of it as long as you can.

The Total System

Your digestive system is strong, hearty, and agreeable. Here's an example of just how good-natured it can be. Suppose you went somewhere for dinner, and first you had some fruit cocktail, served piping hot and smeared with mustard. The main course was a big piece of chocolate cake with tuna-noodle casserole piled on top. Dessert was a scoop of cherry vanilla ice cream covered with a fried egg, runny yolk and all, and a glass of milk to wash it all down, full of salt.

How do you think your digestive system would like that? It wouldn't mind one bit. Your stomach mashes everything into an unrecognizable mush anyway. You want to give it chocolate cake with tuna and noodles? A little weird but okay.

Your digestive system is even very tolerant when you make things difficult, like when you eat a dish of ice cream. Your stomach gets pretty cold then. Usually your stomach is a nice warm 99 degrees F. It may cool as much as 20 degrees from the ice cream. Then it's just too cold to work. Everything stops until it warms up, and you don't even notice. Pepper and mustard make your stomach all fiery and red, but it just keeps mashing.

Sometimes a bubble of gas gets trapped in your small intestine. Either it comes from you swallowing air or it is produced by digestive juices. When the squeezing motion of your intestine hits one of these bubbles, you hear it. Have you ever heard your stomach growl or talk?

Well, the sound isn't coming from your stomach at all; it's that gas bubble in your small intestine. You can explain that next time someone makes a wise-crack about your stomach talking.

Sit back and think about this digestive system of yours. Try to imagine it inside you. The next time you swallow some food, think about how it gets pushed down to your stomach and then gets mashed and moved on to your intestines. Imagine those villi sorting it all out and sending what you need out through your blood stream. It's truly a wonder how your body serves you.

7
You Can Hurt
Your Stomach's Feelings

Even though your digestive system runs on automatic pilot, it's very sensitive to how you feel — especially your stomach. Usually you can tell how a person feels by looking at his or her face. You'd get that same information if you could look at stomachs. Doctors have done this, and they've seen some interesting things.

When you get angry, your stomach gets red. When you're sad or discouraged, it turns pale, gray, and limp. It gets all churned up when you're frustrated, and it just sags when you're disappointed. Sometimes people say they feel too upset to eat. That can be true. Your stomach is as miserable as you are.

Not only do your feelings affect how your stomach looks; feelings can change how the stomach does its job. When all's going well, your stomach keeps working on the food you eat, moving it along

your intestines. If you suddenly become afraid, that fear can cause your stomach to slow down, and then the food moves more slowly. You may feel kind of heavy and sluggish.

If you get angry, the opposite happens. Your stomach speeds up. Your food moves fast — sometimes too fast, and it can get to your intestines too soon, before it's really ready. Then you might have a feeling of indigestion.

When people feel that their stomachs are upset, they usually think that it must have been something they ate. That's not always the case. It could be because of how they're feeling. If you ever do have a stomachache, stop and think about how you're feeling and whether anything has upset you. You may get a clue about where that problem started.

8
How Well Do You Eat?

Here's your chance to take a careful look at your own nutritional habits. What are you really putting into your mouth? What are you choosing to feed those trillions of cells that depend on the food you eat? This is important: The idea of good eating is to get a full assortment of those nutrients your cells need. One way to check on your own assortment is to write down everything you eat and then look at that record carefully.

Try it for the next three days. Three days is a fairer sample than just one.

You'll get better hints about any patterns of what you are and aren't eating.

The first thing you need to do is to make a chart like the one shown. Either a large-sized index card or a sheet of paper is good to use.

The food categories are one way to organize foods into four groups, each with somewhat the same amounts of the nutrients you need. When you use the chart, keep track of how many servings you eat from each group. These descriptions tell you about that.

MY 3-DAY EATING CHART

FOODS	DAY 1	DAY 2	DAY 3	FOODS I DON'T KNOW WHERE TO CHECK
MILK GROUP				DAY 1
PROTEIN GROUP				
VEGETABLE-FRUIT GROUP				DAY 2
BREAD-CEREAL GROUP				DAY 3

WHAT FOODS ARE IN EACH GROUP?

Milk Group. Milk and most foods made from milk are in this group. Each of these counts as about one serving: a glass of milk, three scoops of ice cream, a small carton of yogurt, a cup and a half of cottage cheese, a one-inch cube of hard cheese, a slice of cheese about enough for a sandwich, a medium milkshake.

Vegetable-Fruit Group. Any of these count as a vegetable serving in this group: half a cup of any cooked vegetable, an ear of corn, a potato, a tomato, a green salad, a portion of cole slaw or sauerkraut, an order of French fries, a bowl of vegetable soup. With fruits, a serving would be an apple, orange, banana, peach, pear, nectarine or an average amount of grapes, pineapple, prunes, raisins, plums, or apricots. Half a grapefruit counts as one serving. So does a small glass of orange juice, grapefruit juice, or tomato juice.

Protein Group. All meats are in this group, plus other foods that provide the same nutrients as meat. A serving is one portion of meat, fish, or poultry. That could be a hamburger, two pieces of chicken, a lamb chop, a pork chop, three fish sticks, the meat used to fill two tacos. Two eggs count as one serving. So do about four big spoonfuls of peanut butter, about enough for two sandwiches, or a big handful of nuts.

Bread-Cereal Group. Here is what a serving might be in this group: one slice of bread, a tortilla, half a hamburger or hot dog bun, half an English muffin, a bowl of cooked or dry cereal, half a cup of noodles, rice, spaghetti, or grits, a biscuit, a four-inch pancake, half a waffle, three or four crackers.

Extra Foods. These are foods that don't fit into the other four food groups. You

38

don't keep track of these on your chart, since they don't provide the essentials you need for your nutritional picture. Some examples here are soft drinks, jams, jellies, candy, cakes, gravy, pickles, ketchup, mustard, Jell-O.

Look at this sample breakfast you might eat: two eggs, one glass of milk, two pieces of toast with butter and jelly, one glass of orange juice. Each time you eat a serving in any one of the four food groups, it gets marked on your chart with a check. The eggs in this breakfast count as one serving in the Protein Group and get a check mark there. The glass of milk is one serving in the Milk Group. Two pieces of toast equal two servings in the Bread-Cereal Group. The glass of orange juice is a serving in the Vegetable-Fruit Group. That's all you need to record. Here's what the chart would look like for that breakfast.

FOODS	DAY 1	DAY
MILK GROUP	✓	
PROTEIN GROUP	✓	
VEGETABLE-FRUIT GROUP	✓	
BREAD-CEREAL GROUP	✓✓	

Here's another sample breakfast: cereal, three spoonfuls of sugar on it, one glass of milk, about half a glass of milk extra on the cereal. Check how this breakfast got marked on the sample chart. Notice

how half a check got marked in the Milk Group for the milk on the cereal.

FOODS	DAY 1	DAY
MILK GROUP	✓˱	
PROTEIN GROUP		
VEGETABLE-FRUIT GROUP		
BREAD-CEREAL GROUP	✓	

Do you have your chart made? If not, do it now and you can get started. Think about what you ate for breakfast today. Check each food to see what group it's in and mark it on your chart.

Keep doing this for everything you eat for three days. You'll have to decide how much counts as a serving in some cases. Don't worry too much if you're not sure. The idea here is not to examine exactly how much of everything you eat. The idea is to give you your overall food picture.

NOW LET'S SEE... WHERE DO I MARK SOMETHING MADE OF SODIUM CASEINATE, POLYSORBATE 60, SORBITAN, MONO STEARATE, XANTHAN GUM, GUAR GUM...

COOL WHIP

If you eat something and you don't have the book with you and can't decide where to mark it, then jot it on the back of your chart and check this listing later. If you still can't decide, check with one of your parents to help you make a decision. Tricky foods to mark often come from a combination of groups, spaghetti and meat balls, for example. It gets a check in the Protein Group (the meatballs), a check in the Bread-Cereal Group (the spaghetti), and a check in the Vegetable-Fruit Group (the tomato sauce).

What Your Chart Tells You

After you record on your chart for three days, you'll have a sense of how well rounded your diet is. Are there any empty spaces?

Here's how many servings you need to have for a well-balanced food day:

Milk Group: four servings (three servings are enough if you are under 11 years old).

Protein Group: Two servings.

Vegetable-Fruit Group: Four servings.

Bread-Cereal Group: Four servings.

Take a look at your chart and compare each day with these numbers of servings. Too much extra in any category can mean extra weight eventually. Any categories that are short is a clue to you.

Well, how well do you eat?

40

9
The American Sweet Tooth

There's really not much good to say about sugar. Not everyone thinks that's so. (Do you?) There are lots of people who like sugar. They say it tastes good, and eating would be boring without it.

But that doesn't change the nutritional facts. If you ate no added sugar in any of your foods and cut out sugar-loaded snacks and drinks, your body would do just fine. And it would probably be very grateful for your extra care.

Nutritionally, sugar does only one job. It produces energy. That's it. Sometimes sugar is called the quick-energy food. It's important to know a little about that.

The Quickest of the Quick

All carbohydrates produce energy. Sugar is a carbohydrate, so is starch. Your body uses foods with either sugar or starch in them for fuel to give you energy. The reason sugar is considered to be the quickest energy source is because sugar goes through your digestive system faster than other carbohydrates. And carbohydrates go through faster than any other food.

So if you're hungry and you eat a candy bar, two things may happen. You may not feel hungry anymore, and you may get a spurt of energy soon, within half an hour, as soon as that sugar gets into your blood stream to travel to your cells. So far so good.

There's a catch, though, and a serious one. Your cells can only use so much fuel. When you eat a lot of sugar, even just a candy bar, some of it gets used for fuel. The extra that isn't needed for fuel just then gets changed to fat and stored in your body.

You get a big whoosh of energy all at once. But pretty soon, your fuel is low again, and you're feeling draggy and hungry. Then you may eat another sugary snack and have another zoom up. And then another drop. It's treating your body like a yo-yo.

What you need to eat for energy is a combination of foods that won't rush into your blood stream but will trickle in over a longer period of time. Sugar is too fast. Other carbohydrates, along with fats and proteins, will do your energy needs much more good.

Athletes have to be in top shape. Suppose a tennis player or a long distance runner gobbled some candy bars before the big event. They'd get a spurt of energy part way into the match or race, but then they might experience what's called "sugar crash." There would be a fuel lag later, and they wouldn't feel so hot. There's no use dragging over the finish line after the crowds have all gone home.

Besides producing energy and building up fat in your body, sugar gives no other benefit, not one extra nutritional thing. No vitamins. No minerals. No nothing. It's a single purpose food. Maybe that's what they mean when they write "pure" sugar on the package.

So why do people eat so much of it? Habit. Did you ever get a reward for doing something right when you were a little kid, and it was a sweet treat? Maybe you still do. Sweets get to be thought of as a treat, something special, when you're young. That's how you get started on a sugar habit.

42

A SUGAR TEST

HERE'S SOMETHING FOR YOU TO TRY THAT GIVES YOU A CHANCE TO ACTUALLY FEEL WHAT SUGAR DOES.

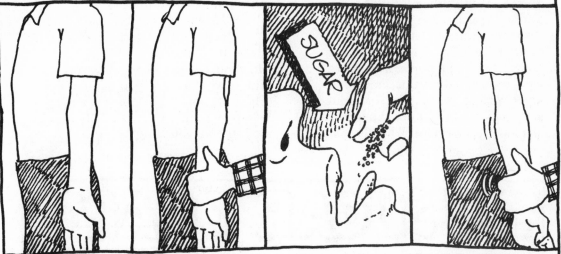

You need a friend or one of your parents or a sister or brother to help out. What you do is stand, arms at your sides, with the palms of your hands facing out and the backs of your hands against your leg.

Have the other person hold your wrist and try to pull your arm away from your body while you do your best to resist. It may or may not be possible for the person to pull your arm up. That's not as important as you feeling how your are able to tighten up your arm muscles and resist the pull. Try this now to get that feeling.

Now the other person will do the same thing again. But first, take a small pinch of sugar, about the amount that you can hold in between your thumb and forefinger. Put that teeny pinch on your tongue and swallow it. Now have the other person pull on your arm again.

What will happen is that you won't be able to resist this second time. Remember, it's not a tug-of-war between the two of you. It's an experiment to help you judge your own ability to use those upper arm muscles with and without the influence of sugar. Right after putting the sugar on your tongue, your arm muscles just won't work for you in the same way.

What's happening here? It's the sugar. Your body is reacting against the sugar in a very special way — you lose strength in your arms — and instantaneously. It's a startling experiment, and it gives you a clue to how your body really feels about sugar.

You might want to try this with someone who is stronger than you are, someone whose arm you couldn't possibly pull away. See if you can do it when they've put that pinch of sugar on their tongue.

The Junk Food Bill

In California, in 1977, a law was proposed that would ban selling certain foods in elementary and junior high schools. It was called the Junk Food Bill. The bill would have banned carbonated drinks, drinks with less than 50 percent full strength fruit juice, candy, Popsicles, and gum with sugar. Also, more nutritional foods would be available for students to buy, like milk and dairy products, fruit juices, nuts, fresh and dry fruits, crackers. The law never passed. The soft drink and candy manufacturers thought that bill was a terrible idea. What do you think of a Junk Food Bill? Is there such a thing in your school or in the state where you live?

How Sweet Is Your Sweet Tooth?

Americans eat over 100 pounds of sugar a year. That's more than a quarter of a pound per person every day, which measures out to be about three-quarters of a cup.

How much sugar do you eat every day? This chart may help you figure it out. There are about 115 grams in a quarter of a pound, the American daily average. So estimate your daily total.

THE SUGAR CHART

1 LEVEL TEASPOON OF WHITE SUGAR	5 GRAMS
1 LEVEL TEASPOON OF BROWN SUGAR	3 GRAMS
1 LEVEL TEASPOON OF SYRUP (FOR PANCAKES)	4.9 GRAMS
1 LEVEL TEASPOON OF HONEY	5.1 GRAMS
1 LEVEL TEASPOON OF JELLY OR JAM	5 GRAMS
1 OUNCE OF CANDY	20 GRAMS
1/2 OUNCE PIECE OF CHOCOLATE	30 GRAMS
1/4 CUP OF RAISINS	20 GRAMS
1 CAN OF COLA (12 OUNCES)	30 GRAMS
1 GLASS OF JUICE DRINK	20 GRAMS
1 SCOOP OF ICE CREAM	12 GRAMS
1 PIECE OF APPLE PIE	20 GRAMS
1 SMALL PIECE OF CAKE OR A CUPCAKE	10 GRAMS

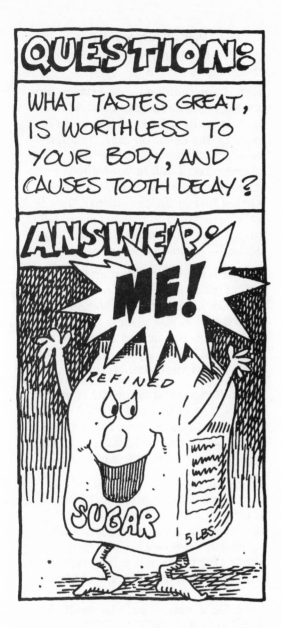

QUESTION:

WHAT TASTES GREAT, IS WORTHLESS TO YOUR BODY, AND CAUSES TOOTH DECAY?

ANSWER:

ME!

REFINED SUGAR 5 LBS.

How much sugar should you eat? There's no exact answer to that one. The average American diet is about 20 percent sugar. Most nutritionists think that should be cut at least in half. Others say cut it down to 5 percent. Still others say cut it out entirely, after all, most fruits and vegetables have sugar in them, and your body is a good enough factory to make its own fuel for energy from the starch, protein, and fats you eat.

The Tooth Decay Story

Yep, that one's true too. Sugar causes tooth decay. Here's how. There are bacteria lurking in your mouth. You know that fuzzy coating on your teeth in the morning when you wake up? That coating is full of fast-growing bacteria. Bacteria are teeny little creatures, and they like your mouth a lot. That's because they like to eat lots of the same things you do, and they get great tidbits from what passes through your mouth and gets lodged in your teeth.

When bacteria digest sugar, acid is produced, and acid is strong stuff. It is strong enough to eat away at the enamel protecting your teeth. Then come cavities and then trips to the dentist.

Queen Elizabeth ruled England in the late 1500s. She ate enough sugar to rot her teeth to black stumps. Imagine that smile!

The best thing you can do is to avoid sugar. The next best thing you can do for your teeth is to keep them well brushed. And the least you can do is rinse after eating.

TRUE LOVE!

Where Does Sugar Come From?

Sugar is manufactured by plants. That's why there's sugar in lots of food that you eat — fruits and vegetables, especially. Plants store sugar in different parts. Some do it in their roots, some in their stems or trunks.

Most of the sugar you buy comes from sugar cane. Sugar cane is a type of grass, and it stores sugar in its stems. At a sugar refinery, the stems are chopped into small pieces and crushed. A juice is produced. The juice is filtered. Then it crystallizes, and this crystallized substance is separated into raw sugar and molasses. The raw sugar gets refined into the sugar that is sold in markets.

The sugar in sugar beets is the same as cane sugar. Beets store sugar in the roots not the stems. About one-fourth of all our sugar comes from sugar beets.

Fructose and glucose are the sugars mostly found in fruits and vegetables. Then there's sucrose. White table sugar is sucrose, so are powdered sugar, brown sugar, and molasses. Galactose is another sugar that isn't found in foods but is manufactured in your body. Lactose is a sugar found in milk. Maltose, or malt syrup, is another sugar, so is corn syrup and maple syrup. Sometimes glucose is called dextrose. Got all that?

When you say you need energy, what you really mean is that your body needs glucose. And your body makes that from many foods, not just from sugar.

You're Surrounded by Sugar

Even if you didn't eat any extra sugary snacks, you'd get plenty of sugar in your daily diet. All you have to do is to check the labels on cans, boxes, or packages of prepared foods from the supermarket. Look in your kitchen cupboard. Examine some labels. If sugar is listed first in the ingredients, then it is the main thing in that product: Jell-O, for instance, juice drinks, some breakfast cereals, some pudding snacks.

If sugar is listed second, then it's the second main ingredient. Check all soda pop, cake mixes, cookies, some cereals. Then see what else sugar is in: soups, hot dogs, bacon, canned fruit, mayonnaise, salad dressings, cans of vegetables, crackers, spaghetti dinners, pizza mixes.

Try to find at least 20 products in your cupboard or in the supermarket that have sugar in them. Remember to read over the list of other names for sugar. Sugar is sugar no matter what name is used.

Sometimes little creatures get into sacks of flour or boxes of pancake mix. It's inevitable, even in the cleanest kitchen cupboard. Everyone has got to eat somewhere. One package is totally safe, however. That's sugar. No worry about bugs or weevils there. They're just not interested. Only humans eat such stuff. Are you sure you should?

10
The Fizz in Your Diet

Soda pop is a big part of many kids' diets. Drinking most soft drinks isn't much different than drinking sugared water with some bubbles and flavoring. How did they get invented? And how did they get so popular?

Joseph Priestley was born in England in 1767. He was a scientist and the person who discovered oxygen. He was serious about his work, but he was known to occasionally clown around in the laboratory. One time he figured out how to make carbonated water. He gleefully put bubbles in water just to entertain

his friends. He died in 1809, after having moved to the United States. He died with no idea of the big fizz he started. Carbonated drinks are now a multimillion dollar industry, with Americans drinking an average of almost 700 bottles of the stuff each year.

There were several people who thought it might be possible to sell water with fizz to a lot of people. The first person to do this was a chemistry professor at Yale who bottled and sold carbonated water in 1807. Several others did the same after him.

47

But it was John Matthews who started carbonated water on its way to the big time. What he bottled and sold in 1832 wasn't much different from the others on the market, but he added another ingredient — advertising. Here's the catchy slogan he used that made it all such a success:

What do you think about that? Well, it worked. John Matthews was a great success, and this was all just for carbonated water. That's water with bubbles only, no flavor added.

It took another fifty years before anyone thought to flavor the drink. No one is quite sure who had that idea, but soda counters began to appear in drugstores and other stores. Flavored soda water caught on quickly. By 1900, lots of bottled soda was sold. The flavors which were favorites included root beer, birch beer, spruce beer, pepsin, ginger, lemon, cola, cherry, sarsaparilla, champagne, and claret. Which of those have you tasted?

Today the most popular flavored drinks are the cola drinks. The first one of those developed was Coca-Cola, and it still out-

sells all its competitors. A druggist in Atlanta, Georgia, invented this concoction in 1886. He was John Pemberton, and he mixed up a brew for the purpose of curing headaches and hangovers. He did this in his backyard, in a big iron kettle, stirring with an oar. He mixed extracts of leaves from the coca tree and nuts from the cola tree. He made 25 gallons of the stuff, and he made a profit of $50 the first year he sold any. It wasn't a soda drink. It was only a syrup with the cola flavor that he made.

John Pemberton probably sold some of his mixture to other druggists, too, because it was another druggist who thought to put some soda water in it. That gave it a bit of zip. Then there was a third druggist, Asa Candler, who suffered from terrible headaches. He liked the cola mixture and especially liked it with the zip of soda water. He figured people would like to drink it for pleasure, not just for medicine. He jumped into the business and bought the recipe from John Pemberton for $2000. That recipe today is figured to be worth $42 million!

It caught on — big. Why? It was a flavor people liked. Good advertising was used. It was an easy name to say and an easy name to remember. Try to think of all the Coke jingles and slogans you can remember. Check with your parents — they may remember some you've never heard. It's spread past the United States. Coca-Cola now sells in 130 countries. Coke is a word that's probably understood in most countries today, and the world drinks over 100 million cokes every day.

What is in this drink that people are so crazy about? Check out the ingredients on a can or bottle: carbonated water, sugar, caramel color, phosphoric acid, natural flavorings, caffeine. That listing means it's mostly carbonated water and sugar. Those two ingredients make up 99 percent of every coke you drink. The natural flavorings are what make up that $42 million secret. It's thought that they include traces of coca and cola (or else they wouldn't use that name), cinnamon, nutmeg, vanilla, lime juice, lavender, citrus oils, glycerin, and a secret ingredient that the company calls 7X.

Coke is terrible stuff for you. You may think it tastes good, but it has no nutritional value whatsoever; it causes tooth decay, and the caffeine in it is a drug that affects your central nervous system. Caffeine is the same drug that's in coffee, and most adults agree that coffee isn't a healthy drink for kids. (It probably isn't good for adults either!)

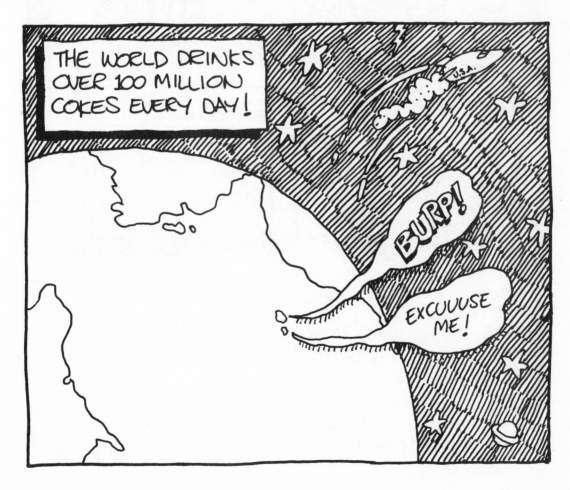

It's not just Coke that's bad. It's all the sugared soda pop. The cola drinks and Dr Pepper are the only ones which add caffeine, but they all share the reputation for being totally nonnutritional. A dental experiment showed that children who drank a can of pop a day for three years suffered 50 to 150 percent more decay in certain teeth than other kids who drank water.

So how come if something is at best useless and at worst harmful, people drink it? It's hard to avoid. You're told about sodas every day in lots of different ways: on TV, on radio, on billboards, on signs in stores. You're constantly urged to try "the pause that refreshes," the "un-cola," "the real thing." How many of those messages do you get in a day? Make a little chart on an index card and keep track for three days so you can see what your average fizzy information record is.

THE BONE IN THE POP EXPERIMENT!

TRY THIS ONE...POUR SOME OF WHATEVER CARBONATED DRINK YOU USE IN A GLASS AND PUT IN A CHICKEN BONE.

LEAVE IT IN FOR A WEEK OR SO AND SEE WHAT HAPPENS TO THE BONE. THEN THINK OF YOUR TEETH. IF YOU CAN GET A TOOTH, TRY THAT INSTEAD OF A BONE. THAT WILL GIVE YOU AN EYEFUL.

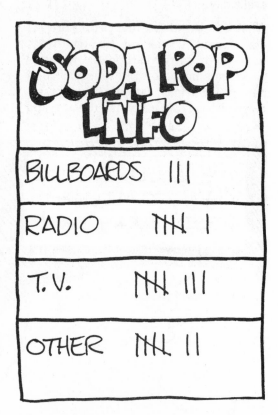

SODA POP INFO

BILLBOARDS	|||
RADIO	|||||	
T.V.	||||| |||
OTHER	||||| ||

The companies that manufacture the stuff feel that they're serving a need — they're making a product that people like to drink. And that's how they make a living too.

But still, you're the one who pours it in and swallows it. And as long as you, and everyone else, buys soda pop, it will still be around. It's up to you to decide how it will fit into your life and diet.

11
Honey: Is It Healthier?

Honey is another form of sugar.

For a long time, people have thought that honey is pretty special stuff. It's been found buried along with Pharaohs in their tombs in ancient Egypt. It's been mentioned in the Bible. It was given to Greek athletes after they had a hard workout. Egyptian bridegrooms were expected to supply their brides with 24 bins of honey at the marriage ceremony. That was about 32 pounds. Honey was supposed to be a good love potion. And it was thought by some to keep people young for a long time.

What Is Honey?

Honey starts out as a thin, watery, sugary fluid. It's called nectar, and it's usually found at the base of flowers. Honeybees are perfectly equipped to remove this nectar. They have long tongues that are hollow, like straws. What a bee does is zoom out of the hive to look for nectar. And it really zooms, traveling at about 35 miles per hour. It travels from flower to flower, collecting just a drop of nectar from each flower through its tongue. Each drop gets put into its honey sac. That's a tiny compartment inside the bee, kind of like a plastic bag. In that little bag, the nectar begins a chemical change to become honey.

People build hives for bees. They're usually wooden boxes. If bees don't have hives, they use caves or hollow trees. Whatever they use for a hive, once inside, bees make honeycomb from wax they produce in their bodies.

When the bee has a full load of nectar, which may be after collecting from 500 to 1,100 blossoms, it heads back to the beehive. Then it's only traveling at about ten miles per hour.

When a bee with a full load of nectar gets back to the hive, it puts that load in one of the compartments in the honeycomb, called a cell. House bees, in the hive, help with this. After the honey is deposited, it begins to ripen, which means that most of the water in the nectar gets evaporated. Meanwhile, the honeybees go off to get more nectar. The house bees stay in the hive, keeping the comb clean and keeping it cool with the air conditioning provided by the fanning of their wings. When the honey is ready, they seal it inside a cell in the comb with a wax cover.

Although bees can live up to six months during the cold winter months, they only live for four or six weeks in the summer. In that short life, a bee collects about one teaspoonful of nectar. This isn't much since it takes four pounds of nectar to make one pound of honey. A strong, average colony of bees numbers about 60,000. This includes both hive bees and those that gather nectar. These 60,000 bees produce a pound of honey — sometimes more, if there are lots of flowers around their hive.

Just think about the work those 60,000 bees do next time you dip into a pound jar or can of honey.

Bees don't do all this work just so you can have some honey when you want it. It's their winter food. When beekeep-ers remove the honey, they're sure to leave enough to get the bees through the winter.

Honey doesn't all taste the same. It depends on what kinds of flowers were used to get the nectar. Clover honey means that the nectar was gathered from clover blossoms. Bees in different parts of the United States use different flowers. You get orange blossom honey from Florida and raspberry honey from New Jersey. There's dandelion honey from Colorado, sage honey from Arizona, tulip tree honey from Maryland. Do you have a favorite honey?

The Honey Argument

Some people think that honey is better to use than sugar. Others disagree. Here's how that argument goes.

Honey is healthier, some say, because it is a natural food with some vitamins in it — minerals too. When sugar is refined, it has no vitamins or minerals at all.

But, others say, the quantity of vitamins and minerals in honey doesn't amount to much. It's still mainly sugar and should be avoided just like any other sugar.

Honey is lots sweeter though, the argument goes on, so you only have to use half as much when you want to sweeten something.

Yes, others say, but it sticks to your teeth more easily than sugar, so it's even a greater danger for tooth decay than plain white sugar.

The argument hasn't been settled. But honey is mainly a pure energy food, with not much additional nutritional value. It shouldn't be filling up a big part of your stomach.

12
Some Tasty Information

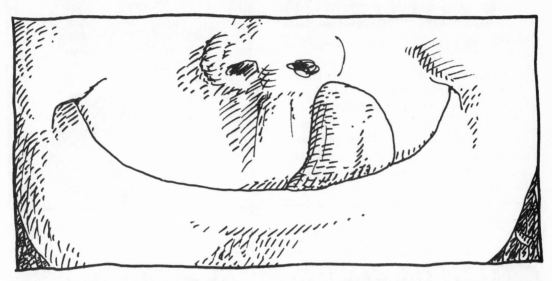

Even though sugar isn't nutritionally very good, most people think that sweet things taste especially good. How come? It's partly your taste buds and partly habit.

When you are born, you have taste buds all over the inside of your mouth. But they don't all last. By the time you are a grownup, most of them will have disappeared. Since kids have more tastebuds than grownups, that may be why some kids are fussier about what they like to eat. When you're an adult, you'll still be left with about 3,000 taste buds, mostly on your tongue. And though that may seem like a lot, it isn't enough to do your tasting for you unassisted.

Lots of the information you get about how something tastes comes from what you smell, or see, or touch too. Have you ever come home and when you walked in, you smelled something cooking in the kitchen? You knew just what it was from the smell, and you imagined taking a taste. Can you do that?

Your sense of smell tells you a lot about how something tastes. Here's a way to test that for yourself.

THE ORANGE AND GRAPEFRUIT TEST

YOU NEED A GLASS OF ORANGE JUICE AND ONE OF GRAPEFRUIT JUICE. TASTE THEM TO MAKE SURE YOU CAN TELL THE DIFFERENCE. NOW CLOSE YOUR EYES AND HOLD YOUR NOSE, SO YOU CAN'T SMELL ANYTHING. HAVE SOMEONE ELSE, A FRIEND OR PARENT, GIVE YOU ONE TO TASTE. ARE YOU SO SURE WHICH IT IS?

YUMMY VANILLA!

Sometimes your sense of smell can fool your sense of taste. Try this. Look in the cupboard for a bottle of vanilla. Open the bottle and take a sniff. Vanilla is a flavoring used in lots of cakes and cookies and, of course, in ice cream. Do you like that smell? Now, put a drop of vanilla on your little finger and taste it. How was that? Was it what you expected?

YOUR SALIVA HAS AN EFFECT ON HOW YOU TASTE. HERE'S A WAY TO LEARN ABOUT THAT.

THE WET AND DRY TASTE TEST

WIPE TONGUE DRY...

A GARBANZO BEAN?

PLACE SUGAR CUBE...

MOISTEN TONGUE

SUGAR!

SUGAR CUBE AGAIN...

For this experiment, you'll need another person to be the taster. Ask the taster to wash their mouth with water and then wipe their tongue with a tissue until it's dry. Have the taster keep their mouth open and tongue extended, so the taste buds don't get wet again.

Ask the taster to hold their nose and close their eyes. Then you put a sugar cube or a candy mint on their tongue. (Don't tell what the food is!) Leave it there for thirty seconds and then remove it. Ask them what they tasted.

Now try the same test again, but this time the taster's tongue should be moist. Put the sugar cube or mint on the same part of the tongue that you did before. Wait 30 seconds. Remove it, and ask your taster what that taste was like. Try this test with other foods too. And try being the taster yourself for a first-hand experience.

There are only four basic tastes: sweet, sour, bitter, and salty. Most foods are a combination of some of these tastes. The one that appears most is sometimes easy to pick out, sometimes not. A chocolate bar is sweet. That's because of the sugar and that taste is easy to identify. What about an apple? Is it sweet, sour, bitter, or salty? What about a banana? Peanut butter? Mustard? What can you think of that is bitter?

How would you classify the vanilla you tasted?

The taste buds on the tip of your tongue are the ones that taste sweet things. Going back from the tip along the sides are the taste buds for salty things. The ones farther back on the sides of your tongue are most sensitive to sourness, and the ones at the back of your tongue, to bitterness.

There are lots of other words that are used to describe how things taste besides sweet, sour, bitter, or salty. How about bread tasting "fresh"? Or a taco tasting "spicy"? Cinnamon candy or gum tastes

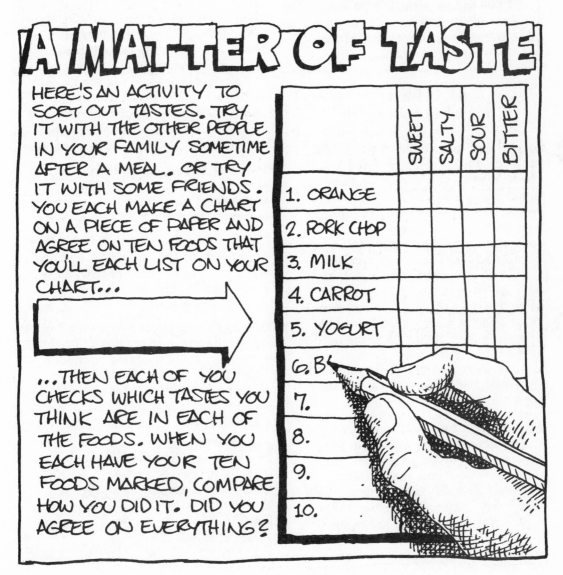

A MATTER OF TASTE

HERE'S AN ACTIVITY TO SORT OUT TASTES. TRY IT WITH THE OTHER PEOPLE IN YOUR FAMILY SOMETIME AFTER A MEAL. OR TRY IT WITH SOME FRIENDS. YOU EACH MAKE A CHART ON A PIECE OF PAPER AND AGREE ON TEN FOODS THAT YOU'LL EACH LIST ON YOUR CHART...

...THEN EACH OF YOU CHECKS WHICH TASTES YOU THINK ARE IN EACH OF THE FOODS. WHEN YOU EACH HAVE YOUR TEN FOODS MARKED, COMPARE HOW YOU DID IT. DID YOU AGREE ON EVERYTHING?

	SWEET	SALTY	SOUR	BITTER
1. ORANGE				
2. PORK CHOP				
3. MILK				
4. CARROT				
5. YOGURT				
6. B				
7.				
8.				
9.				
10.				

"hot," and other candies and gum taste "fruity." Check the food ads you see on TV or on signs and the labels on foods in your cupboard or in stores. See what words are used to describe the tastes of different foods. See how many of those descriptions you agree with.

Did you know that there are people who are official tasters. That's their job. They work for food companies tasting new products. Some of the good tasters earn more than $30,000 a year. There's a company in Massachusetts that has trained over 1,000 tasters in the last 20 years. Maybe they should get kids to do that job. After all, you've got more of those taste buds that you were born with.

It's All What
You're Used To

Lots of what tastes good to you is what you're used to. If you were given lots of sweets when you were little, then you probably like sweets a lot. Many people have gotten used to drinking skimmed milk. They may think it tastes better than whole milk, just because they're used to it. Ask a grown-up who drinks alcohol, like scotch or other whiskey. Ask them if they can remember the first time they had some. That should be a pretty good story. Be sure to ask them if they liked the taste the first time they tried it. Lots of people have developed tastes for some kinds of alcohol, but they usually didn't start out thinking it was just terrific.

What is tasty to you can be yucky to someone else. In some schools in the southwestern part of the United States, the kids get noontime snacks called *saladitos*. A saladito is half a lemon with a very, very salty prune jammed in the middle. The prune flavors the lemon. You eat it by pushing down on the prune to loosen the juice in the lemon.

Then you suck out some of that juice. It's real salty and real lemony. Do you think you'd like it?

Some people eat other things you might never have thought about trying. French people eat both snails and frogs' legs, though many people who aren't French eat them too. Sheep's eyes are a special Arab treat. There's a Chinese soup called birds' nest soup. It's actually made from nests of birds called *swiftlets*. They lay their eggs on a soft bed made from their own saliva.

There are gypsies in Great Britain who eat hedgehogs. They bake them in clay. That way, when they peel off the clay to eat them, the spines and skins come off too. Hedghogs are said to taste like pig. Japanese people eat raw fish, called *sashimi*. Iguana meat is eaten in Central and South America. Just the back of the iguana is cooked, fixed in a casserole.

Have you ever been to a friend's or relative's house and seen or smelled food that seemed very strange? How did you feel about tasting it? Did you taste it?

Can you tell by a person's face whether or not they like the taste of something? When you taste something new, do you think someone else can tell if you like it by watching your face?

One way to try to develop a taste for something new is to try just a little bit at a time. No use shocking your poor taste buds with a big mouthful. You might be surprised at what you can learn to enjoy eating or drinking starting with nibbles or sips.

56

13

Bread: Food for Everyone's Taste

There are some foods that seem to taste good to people all over the world. Bread for one.

If you asked some kids what their favorite foods were, they might not mention bread in the top three. But it would probably be there. Hamburgers are usually eaten on bread in the form of a bun. Hot dogs, too. Pizza is a flat bread with stuff on top. It's hard to get through a day without eating bread.

That's a good thing. Bread is one of the basics of a well-balanced diet, and it has been for a long time. The Egyptians are given the credit for first making bread like bread is made today. What the Egyptians did was to use the foam from beer they made to make the bread rise. That foam was full of yeast, and yeast is what's used today to make bread rise too. The Egyptians did this 6,000 years ago.

Both bread and beer were very important to the Egyptians, so important that they sometimes used them for money, before coins were invented. Have you ever heard anyone today refer to money as bread?

The Breads You Buy

In different parts of the United States, bakeries make different kinds of breads. There is corn bread, rye bread, pumpernickel bread, potato bread, French bread, Italian bread, sourdough bread. Mexican bakeries sell tortillas, made from corn or flour. Some places, you can buy pita bread, a Syrian pocket bread good for stuffing.

Some people bake their own bread at home. It's a wonderful treat to smell bread baking and then to cut into a freshly baked loaf. Have you ever done that? Maybe you could learn to bake bread. Check in the library for a book — maybe especially for kids — that tells you an easy way to make bread. Or find someone, who knows how, to teach you.

Then there are the breads you can buy in the supermarket. Usually there's an entire aisle with breads on the shelves. Many of those breads are white breads. They're the biggest selling loaves in the store, and that's too bad — nutritionally.

In order to make that white bread, the wheat that is grown has to be processed

— milled, it's called. When it's milled, at least 20 of the nutrients usually found in whole grain wheat are removed. If you'll look on a package of that bread, it probably says "enriched." That means that some of the nutrients have been put back, artificially. But only about 4 or 5 of them. It's just not all it could be.

You may be used to the taste and texture of white bread. But it just is not as nutritious as whole grain breads.

Bread Beliefs

People have believed many things about bread, like it's bad luck to turn a loaf upside-down or to cut an unbaked loaf. Some people thought that if you cut a loaf of bread at both ends, the devil would fly over your house. There was a time when people left bread and coffee under the house to prevent ghosts from coming inside. Some people believed that eating bread would cure whooping cough. Others thought that if a crumb of bread dropped out of your mouth, you would be dead in a week or that whoever ate the last piece of bread from a loaf would have to kiss the cook. Do you know any others?

Without bread, there would be no sandwiches. And without sandwiches, kids' sack lunches would be a whole different story.

HOW MANY DISHES CAN YOU THINK OF THAT USE BREAD AS A MAIN PART? ...LIKE PIZZA, TACOS, OR FRENCH TOAST...

The sandwich was the bright idea of a man named John Montagu. He lived in England around 200 years ago in a place called Sandwich. He was a politician and was known to be a terrible politician. At one point in his career, he was the First Lord of the Admiralty, and because of him the British Navy was in a terrible mess.

He was also a gambler. He liked to gamble so much that he hated to leave the gambling table, even for meals. That's when his bright idea came in handy. If I just put some meat between two slices of bread, he thought, then I can eat and gamble at the same time. So he did.

People thought that was definitely weird, maybe even bad manners. But then again, John Montagu was thought to be a gentleman, with an official title — the Fourth Earl of Sandwich — so no one said anything about it, and pretty soon others were doing it too.

WHAT IF YOU WERE THE EARL OF YOUR TOWN AND YOU INVENTED THE SANDWICH... WHAT WOULD WE CALL THE SANDWICH THEN?

HEY, MOM.... CAN I HAVE A PEANUT BUTTER AND JELLY JACKSON HOLE?

Think how far the sandwich has come today. There's no end to the possibilities. Do you know what a Dagwood sandwich is? If not, ask your parents if they know.

How many sandwiches do you think you eat in a week? Make a guess. Then keep track. Check with your friends too. Who is the biggest sandwich eater you know? What is the funniest or oddest thing you can think of to put in a sandwich?

14
Do You Know Your Noodles?

Noodles are another one of those foods that seem to get along easily with everyone's taste buds.

Have you ever met a kid who didn't like noodles? That would be a hard kid to locate, maybe because noodles have a mild taste that doesn't upset all those extra taste buds kids have that grownups have lost. Or maybe it's because they're fun to eat — if you can get away with slurping them at the dinner table.

Most people believe that the Italians are the ones who started the noodle craze in the world. They did help spread the word about how terrific noodles are, but they didn't invent them.

There are different stories about where noodles first came from. One story says that it was one of the treasures that Marco Polo brought back to Italy when he was off exploring in Asia, about 700 years ago.

Another story says that wasn't the way it was at all. There were fierce tribes that invaded Italy before Marco Polo's time. The cook of one of these tribes was a woman. She fell in love with an Italian man, and one of the gifts she gave him to show her true love was the secret of how to make noodles. Whichever story is true, the Italians must be grateful. They eat a lot of noodles.

SOME NOODLES

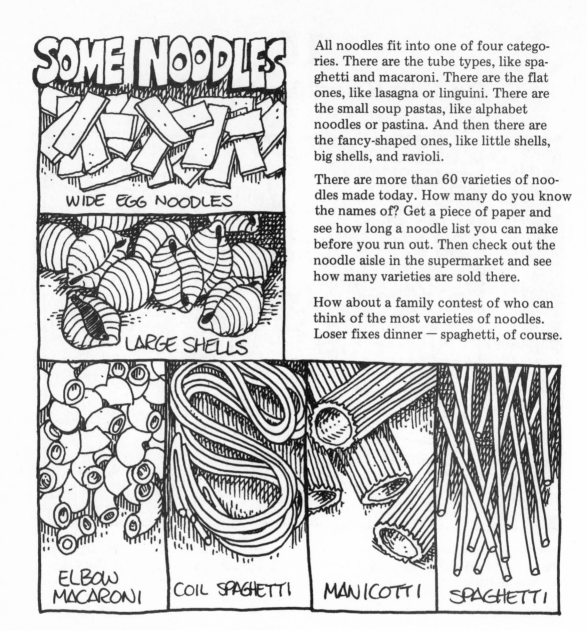

WIDE EGG NOODLES

LARGE SHELLS

ELBOW MACARONI

COIL SPAGHETTI

MANICOTTI

SPAGHETTI

All noodles fit into one of four categories. There are the tube types, like spaghetti and macaroni. There are the flat ones, like lasagna or linguini. There are the small soup pastas, like alphabet noodles or pastina. And then there are the fancy-shaped ones, like little shells, big shells, and ravioli.

There are more than 60 varieties of noodles made today. How many do you know the names of? Get a piece of paper and see how long a noodle list you can make before you run out. Then check out the noodle aisle in the supermarket and see how many varieties are sold there.

How about a family contest of who can think of the most varieties of noodles. Loser fixes dinner — spaghetti, of course.

60

15
The National Meal in a Bun

Then there's the hamburger. That's another food that seems to be a general taste favorite, especially in the United States.

Americans like hamburgers. Regular hamburgers, cheeseburgers, barbeque-burgers, pizzaburgers. About 30 to 40 billion hamburgers are bought at hamburger stands each year. In addition are the ones you fix at home and the fancier ones called chopped sirloin steaks in some restaurants.

In California, they put mayonnaise, lettuce, and tomato on them. In New York, that would be revolting. Onion, maybe. Mustard or ketchup, okay. But mayonnaise, never. How about where you live?

All together, Americans eat over 11 billion pounds of hamburger a year. That's about 55 pounds per person. It's practically the national meal. It wasn't an American idea, though.

The Start of Hamburgers

The Tartars are the people who got the hamburger idea started. They are a people from Central Asia who headed west in the thirteenth century and overran Russia. They were always on the move, herding their sheep. When they stopped to eat, they would kill a sheep for food and scrape little pieces of meat from it. They'd put these pieces in a mound and eat it. Raw.

Have you ever heard of steak tartare? It's served in restaurants today and is a mound of raw meat, chopped beef, not sheep. Check in a cookbook or on a restaurant menu, next time you get the chance.

When the Tartars invaded Russia, the Russians learned about this food custom. They thought it was a super idea and began fixing it too.

The idea kept traveling. There were German towns across the Baltic Sea from

Russia. Sea trading went on in those northern German towns. So the Tartar custom sailed across with the sea traders from Russia and traveled to the German town of Hamburg.

The Germans liked the idea too. They added to it. They added onions, pickles, salted anchovies. They even took to dropping a raw egg yolk on top of the mound. (Have you checked those cookbook recipes yet? You may find one that calls for the egg yolk too.)

Then someone in Germany got a bright idea. Why don't we cook it? And they did. Nice and crusty on the outside, juicy on the inside. They were called *Deutches beefsteak*.

When German people came to the United States, so did the hamburger. It was introduced in this country in 1904, at the St. Louis World's Fair. From that time on, the hamburger boom took off and grew and grew.

The first hamburger chain was started in 1921. It was called the White Castle, and they sold two-and-a-half-inch squares of hamburger for five cents.

The hamburger got even more publicity in the 1930s. The Popeye comic strip was a popular one, and the hamburger was the favorite dish of Popeye's friend, J. Wellington Wimpy.

Besides being a popular food, hamburgers have become big business in our country. Lots of hamburger chains have been started since the White Castle. McDonald's is the biggest, with over 4,000 stands in the United States and foreign countries too. Hamburgers in all of these McDonald's stands are prepared to the same standards. Each is .221 inch thick, 3.875 inches in diameter, weighs 1.6 ounces, takes 55 seconds to put together, and if it isn't sold in ten minutes, it's thrown away. The Tartars could never have imagined that their mounds of meat would become such precision affairs.

Do you know what the biggest number of hamburgers anyone ever ate at one sitting is? Give that a thought. In 1976, someone ate 17 hamburgers in 30 minutes! Quite a mouthful.

What's your hamburger quota? How many do you eat? Do you know? Keep a tally for a week and see. Do you know who eats the most hamburgers? Organize your friends and ask them all to keep their statistics and see how you all shape up.

Could you live on hamburgers? Nope. As a food, they are okay to eat, but they're not a well-balanced diet. Most of the hamburger chains usually sell only hamburgers, French fries, shakes, and desserts. No other vegetables, besides potatoes, and no fruits are available. That's not good for you if you're eating meals there as a steady diet.

I MAY TASTE REALLY GOOD BUT YOU NEED MY FRIENDS HERE TO HELP ROUND OUT YOUR DIET!

...AS WELL AS FRUITS AND DAIRY PRODUCTS.

16
Apple Facts

Apples are another example of a food most people like. Maybe that's because there are so many kinds of apples, it would be hard not to find one to like.

There are about 7,000 varieties of apples. That's how many the United States Department of Agriculture lists, but you don't find that many in your local store. Eight different varieties make up three-fourths of all the commercially grown apples in this country.

How many different apples can you name? How many have you tasted? The favorite apple in the United States is the Red Delicious. The others that are grown most are the McIntosh, Golden Delicious, Rome Beauty, Jonathan, Winesap, York, and Stayman.

No doubt you've heard of Johnny Appleseed. He was a bit of an apple fanatic. His real name was John Chapman, but not too many people would recognize him by that name. He was a tall man, a bit wild-eyed at times. He is usually pictured roaming about with a bag of apple seeds on his shoulder, spreading

them about. Well, he might have been a little strange, but he knew his apples. And he knew you didn't go around just scattering apple seeds and expect to get good results. He carefully planted young trees in nurseries, starting at the Atlantic coast and heading west. He got as far as Indiana before he died in 1845.

HOW MANY DIFFERENT DISHES CAN YOU THINK OF THAT FEATURE APPLES?

Have you ever heard of Henderson Lewelling? He did as much for apples as Johnny Appleseed did. Henderson Lewelling came to Oregon in 1847 in a covered wagon with his wife, children, and 700 fruit trees. All were under four feet tall — except for him and his wife.

His wife and children were happy when the trip was over. Henderson Lewelling took such good care of those trees on the trip that they got watered every day first thing. And he gave only water that was left to the family.

The trees he carried weren't just apple trees, either. They were pear, quince, plum, and cherry trees, too, and he finally got them all planted.

His first crop of ripened apples was a big event. There were 100 apples in all. It was the time of the Gold Rush in California, and when he rushed to San Francisco with his crop, prospectors were so hungry for fresh fruit that he sold those apples for $5 each. He used the money to build up more orchards.

Henderson Lewelling worked with grafted trees, not by planting trees from seedlings. If you plant seeds, even from the same tree, you'll get trees that are all different. But by grafting different cuttings from one tree onto the trunks of other trees, you can reproduce the same apples over and over.

Because of Henderson Lewelling's efforts, apple growing spread north from Oregon. Today the state of Washington produces more apples than any other state.

What's your favorite apple? Take a poll and see what the favorites are of the people you know. You may be surprised how many favorites aren't in the big eight. Some people are dedicated to Pippins or Granny Smith's. Others think Baldwin is the best, and then there are the Northern Spy, the Grimes Golden, the Rhode Island Greening, the Gravenstein. Be careful not to insult anyone's choice. Some people have strong feelings about their apples.

17
Food, Food, Everywhere

It seems so easy today to get any of the foods you like. It wasn't always that way. A long time ago, people ate what they could find. Sometimes what they found was running or flying or — with luck — just wandering around. Maybe it was even swimming, if they lived near water. Food gathering took most of people's time. While hunting, they tasted whatever they found growing: roots, berries, leaves, fruits. They probably spit out lots of what they tasted too.

That all changed. Instead of chasing animals for food, people figured out how to herd them together, and eventually animals were domesticated. Instead of rummaging around eating what they could find growing, people noticed that new plants grew where other plants dropped their seeds. So they started planting the seeds themselves. So then food became available more easily and in more quantity.

Once people did not have to spend all their time finding what they needed to eat, things changed even more. Not everyone had to raise animals for food or to plant seeds for food. Some of the people could do it for the others.

That's the way it is now. Today in the United States, some people have never even seen food growing. Some people wouldn't recognize a broccoli plant if it were right underfoot. Would you?

Most of what people eat today, they buy in stores, usually in supermarkets. And that's all handled for you by the food industry. The food industry is the largest industry in the United States. It includes farming and ranching operations, picking and cutting and wrapping and canning and other processing of food, shipping the food to different places, advertising, and running supermarkets and stores where food is sold.

How this all happened in the United States is quite a story.

In the early 1800s, a general food store sold less than 100 things. That's not much when compared with today's supermarkets which have about 8,000 things you can buy. Also, they wouldn't always have the same things to sell then. There would be vegetables and fruits from the nearby farms. You didn't get tomatoes all year. You got them when they were ripe near where you lived.

Stores would also sell staple foods, like flour, sugar, butter, cheese, tea, and coffee. The way it worked was that the store would stock a big amount of an item, like a bin of flour, and when you wanted to buy some, the person in the store would scoop out just the amount you wanted. People lived mostly in small towns, and part of shopping was chatting with the storekeeper and catching up on local news.

How You Got to Eat Pineapple

Things began to change slowly. Take the tin can, for example. It came along and changed lots of things.

In the nineteenth century, machines were invented to make cans and seal them. All through the 1800s, the canning business grew and grew. By 1900 Americans were totally sold on buying food in cans.

This is how people got to eat foods they never would have been able to try. That's where pineapple comes in. There was plenty of pineapple for you, if you lived in Hawaii. But there was none to. be found in Minnesota. Cans made it possible for pineapple to travel. What things do you eat you never could have without the invention of the tin can? Go and check the kitchen cupboard.

Here's a little tin-can quiz for you. What canned vegetables are Americans' favorites today? And what canned fruits? Which do you think? Well, corn is first in vegetables, with green beans, tomatoes, and peas following. Peaches are the most popular canned fruit, followed by applesauce and then pineapple.

They Began to Sell Convenience

People started to think of other ways to sell foods. Just before 1900, a 25-year-old man who lived in Sharpsburg, Pennsylvania, had an idea. He grew horseradish in his backyard. He began putting it into bottles and selling it to store owners. And the store customers bought it, which cheered up the store owners, which inspired this inventive man to do even more. He began putting pickles in jars, too, and then ketchup and then different kinds of relishes. Pretty convenient for shoppers. Pretty soon he had 57 different items to sell to grocers. That man was named Henry J. Heinz.

In Chicago there was a grocery clerk who thought of a helpful service to provide. He would cut chunks from the enormous store-sized mounds of cheese and wrap them in tinfoil. He got a horse and wagon, loaded up the chunks of cheese, and sold them door-to-door. His name was J. H. Kraft.

If you check the supermarket, you'll be able to see what things the Heinz Company and the Kraft Company are selling now. Maybe you have some of their products in your house right now. Check the cupboards again and the refrigerator too.

Packaging came along for other things too. Salt, for example: salt used to be sold in cotton bags. Sometimes the bag cost more than the salt did. When the weather was damp, the salt got all caked together. Now it's packed in a cardboard box that is lined with waxed paper, and it doesn't get all stuck together in one lump anymore.

So much is packaged today, it's easy not even to notice. A tea bag is a package for a cup of tea. A stick is a way to package a lollipop. A tube of flexible metal is a way to package toothpaste. A cone is a way to package ice cream. Aluminum foil and plastic wrap are ways to package things at home. Cardboard boxes are used for lots of things; plastic bags, for noodles. Bottles and jars are used. Flat-bottomed paper bags that are used to carry groceries home have been made since 1870.

Packaging Helped to Change the Stores

Packaging made things easier for store-keepers. They didn't have to spend their time weighing out five pounds of sugar or half a pound of cheese. Packaging made things easier for shipping food. Stores could stock more things since they were easier to fit on the shelves all packaged. They lasted longer too.

This all worked well for people. Not only were the ways food got packaged and sold changing, the whole country was changing. People were moving to cities. Women began to get jobs, too, instead of staying home and spending all their time doing the cooking and housekeeping chores. Refrigerators became standard home equipment. Cars became more popular. People moved more and moved faster.

They didn't go to the grocery store to chat with the owner while they bought what they needed. They went to the grocery store to get what they needed. Then they stopped at the butcher shop, the fish store maybe, the bakery, and they went on home. Besides, as towns got bigger and cities grew, people didn't always know the store owners anyway.

More and more food manufacturers started to make more and more foods available to stores. Along with packaging came new ways to use those packages. People began to put information on the packages and tried to make them look really snappy so you would be encouraged to buy their flour instead of some other manufacturer's flour. Advertising, it's called. Take Popeye, for example. It's hard to think of Popeye and not think of spinach. What about Chiquita Banana? She's not a real person.

She was made up just to sell more bananas, and she did. Americans eat more bananas than any other fruit, about 18 pounds of bananas per person each year. If you can't sing her song, ask your mom or dad if they know it.

Remember, the average human stomach holds just about *two quarts*. And there are lots of things to buy to fill it up. So there's lots of competition to sell what will fill up that space.

18
The Spread of Supermarkets

With more foods being available, stores got bigger and bigger. The first supermarkets opened in the early 1930s. By the middle of 1955, supermarkets were doing half of all the food selling in the United States. At that time the average supermarket had about 3,000 products to sell.

Some supermarkets sell even more than today's average of 8,000 items. Some stock up to 20,000 items. It's possible to make that one stop and do all the shopping you need for an entire week and even for longer, if you freeze things at home.

You can find foods in your supermarket from lots of different countries: coffee from South American countries and Africa, teas from China and India, products from Japan, France, Portugal, and other countries too. You can choose from 15 flavors of ice cream and sherbet. You can find juice in cans, in bottles, frozen, or in powder to mix with water.

There's whole milk, low-fat milk, skimmed milk, nonfat powdered milk, evaporated milk, buttermilk, condensed milk. You can buy dozens of different kinds of soups and cheeses. There are jams and jellies in every imaginable flavor. It is truly amazing.

It's gotten so that people take all this plenty for granted. If you went into a supermarket, and they said, sorry, they were all out of ice cream or canned soup, you'd probably think that the store owner had also run out of brains or that maybe it was a national emergency. Supermarkets are lots different than the old stores where you reached into the barrel for a pickle or wondered when the lettuce was coming in.

There's more too. In some supermarkets you can rent a machine to clean your rugs, buy plants for your house, magazines and books to read, clothing to wear, even an ice chest to keep the food in, if you're going on a picnic. The store is there to serve any need the shopper might think of while there.

The shopping cart helped with this. There was a time when shoppers brought along their own baskets or carts. Then a clever man got a good idea. Let's give them a carrier for their baskets that they can wheel around the market. If they're not carrying it all the time, they won't notice how heavy it is getting, and they'll put more in it. Then he got even more clever. Let's put our baskets on the carts. We can put bigger baskets on them that way. They'll hold more things, and the shoppers will fill them up like they do their own baskets. It worked. And that man is a rich man today.

Supermarket Psychology

Stores advertise sales every week. Sometimes, the things they have on sale are being sold as "loss leaders." That means that they'll sell them at a loss of money hoping to get shoppers into the store. And then they hope to tempt you to buy lots more.

There's also a lot of thought as to where things get placed in the supermarket. Studies have shown that most things that get bought are on the shelves be-

tween the shoppers' waists and shoulders — no stooping or reaching. Manufacturers all like to have their products on those shelves, unless what they're selling is something little kids like a lot, like cookies or candy. Then those lower shelves are valuable. It's amazing what kids will pick up and put in the cart hoping their mothers or fathers will cheerfully buy them. Have you ever done this?

Those items kept right near the front of the aisles and near the cash registers also sell well. Those are the places for what are called "impulse items." There you are, waiting to have your basketful rung up, just standing there, kind of weary and bored. Then what pops into focus right in front of the basket? A delicious looking jar of dry roasted peanuts. A jar of exotic and expensive olives. A can of smoked oysters that you'd usually never buy, but don't they look interesting right now? A row of tempting candy and chewing gum.

Little is left to chance in the supermarket. Shoppers have to be very, very crafty. It takes a sharp eye and a clear mind to get in there and buy what you need and pay the fairest price. You can start learning about this right now.

Here's a supermarket investigation that you can do. Read it over, maybe with your mom or dad or whoever is going to the supermarket to do the shopping next. Then you can go along and do the information finding while they're shopping, then report the results after you get home.

There are lots of things to investigate, more than you could do in one trip. So pick just a few to try the first time.

Try to guess what you think the results will be before you go. That way you can get a hint as to what your supermarket savvy is now.

THE SUPERMARKET INVESTIGATION

1. Some products in the supermarket come from other countries. How many countries do you think? Name as many as you can.

2. How many different breakfast cereals are sold there? How many of these are sugared? (You can tell by checking the ingredients on the label to see if sugar is added.)

3. Which products do you think will be on the shelves that little kids can reach? List ten. Then check them out.

4. How many flavors of ice cream can you buy in quarts or half gallons, not counting ice cream sandwiches and bars?

5. What kinds of things are sold in the bins nearest the cash register, the "impulse items"?

6. List all the nonfood products you can think of that are sold in your supermarket. Then check your list.

7. List ten foods sold in containers that are reused in your home instead of just thrown away. Find them in the market. What other reusable containers can you find there?

8. How many different sized (not shaped) jars of peanut butter can you buy?

9. Which olives are the biggest: large, jumbo, colossal, giant, extra-large?

10. Super hard: Which food traveled the farthest to get to the store?

19

Have You Ever Tasted a Home-Grown Tomato?

There are still some things you can't buy in the supermarket. A home-grown tomato, for example. Some people say that one of the all-time taste treats is to pick a ripe, home-grown tomato off the vine and bite in. Have you ever tasted one?

That's not possible to do all the time, just when the tomato plants you grow are ready. But you'll notice in the supermarket that you can get tomatoes almost any time of the year. How do they manage that?

First of all, tomatoes can be planted in warmer climates or in greenhouses all year around. Then instead of letting the tomatoes ripen on the vine, the tomato growers who sell to the supermarkets and stores pick them green. That way they won't spoil when they are shipped over long distances.

Tomatoes are usually red when you buy them though. That's because they've been treated with ethylene gas to ripen them and turn them red. Some people think this is a terrible practice. There's disagreement as to whether or not the ethylene gas makes the tomatoes unhealthy for you to eat. But there's not much disagreement that the tomatoes aren't as tasty as they could be. At least, nothing like home-grown ones.

The tomato has seen a few other changes for the sake of shipping. They are now grown with tougher skins. Since they're picked mechanically, tough skins protect them from getting bruised or squished.

It's been said that people have been working on developing square tomatoes that won't waste so much space when they're packed and shipped. Keep an eye out; they may be along soon.

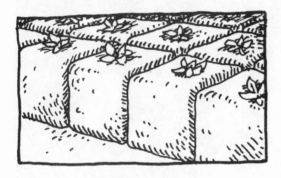

The First Bite

For a long time no one ate tomatoes. They were first found growing in South America, and none of the Indians there seemed interested in eating them. They were brought to Europe by Spanish explorers in the sixteenth century, but Europeans weren't willing to bite in either. People in Spain, Portugal, France, Italy, and England planted them but only for decoration. They thought tomatoes were poisonous since the plant belongs to the same family of plants as the deadly nightshade, which is poisonous.

Tomatoes were planted in the United States too. Thomas Jefferson was said to be the first person to plant one. That was in 1781. But there were still no takers for eating them.

A tomato lover changed all that. He was Robert Gibbon Johnson, and he was devoted to the tomato, for sure. One day this fearless man stood on the steps of the Salem County Courthouse in New Jersey and ate a tomato — right there in front of shocked spectators. He ate it. They waited. And watched. And waited. Robert seemed just fine. And he lived to go on and eat lots more.

As a result of that daredevil feat, the tomato is now a commonplace food in American homes.

P.S. Have you heard that the tomato is not a vegetable? Actually, the tomato is the fruit of the plant. But you eat tomatoes as vegetables in the main part of your meal, not as a light snack or dessert. No matter, anyway. They are a terrific food, with plenty of vitamins and minerals. If you've never tasted a home-grown one, keep a lookout. You may get your chance someday.

20
The Invention of Foods

Hundreds of new foods are introduced in supermarkets each year. You eat foods now that no one ever thought of 100 or so years ago. You even eat some that weren't around 10 years ago. Chew that over for a minute.

Here's the start of a list of invented foods: breakfast cereals, margarine, Jell-O, carbonated soda, peanut butter, Oreo cookies, potato chips, TV dinners, alphabet noodles, frozen yogurt, instant mashed potatoes, Popsicles, ice cream sandwiches, candy bars, pretzels, Hawaiian Punch, Kool-Aid, frozen pizza, chili dogs, imitation mayonnaise, imitation sour cream, ice milk. The list can go on and on and on. Think of what other foods you could add to it.

Is There Any Peanut Butter in Your House?

Americans eat a lot of peanut butter. Four out of every five American cupboards have a jar of peanut butter in them. How about your house? Do you think this is true for the people you know? Do you think kids like peanut butter more than grownups? Ask around and see what you can learn.

Peanut butter was invented in 1890 by a doctor who lived in St. Louis. He developed it to be an easily digested high-protein food. And it is high protein. Two tablespoons of peanut butter will provide you with 8 grams of the 44 grams you need of protein every day, along with some vitamins and minerals.

When peanut butter was first sold, grocers ladled it out to customers from big tubs. First they had to stir it. Have you ever noticed that your peanut butter needs stirring? There's nothing wrong with it; it's just the oils separating out. Some peanut butters have stabilizers added, so the oils don't do this.

Once lots of different food manufacturers got into the peanut butter business, some government regulations were set. One is that all peanut butter has to be at least 90 percent peanuts. That was no easy decision. It was made in 1970 by the Supreme Court of the United States, the highest court in the country. That was 11 years after the regulation was first proposed. There was some hassle. Some of the peanut butter makers felt they could make just as good peanut butter with less peanuts. Other concerned peanut butter lovers said that was ridiculous. But today, 90 percent of the peanut butter must consist of peanuts. That's the law.

Here's how peanut butter is made. Spanish peanuts are used. They're roasted at about 300 degrees F for about 20 minutes. They're cooled quickly, and then the skins are removed. Then they're ground up, usually twice. Anything extra that is added, is added the second time they're ground. Usually salt is added. Some brands add sweetener or some hardened oil to keep the spread from separating. Check the peanut butter in your cupboard to see what's in it besides peanuts.

What kind is your favorite, chunky or smooth? What about your favorite peanut butter sandwich — just peanut butter, with jelly, honey, bananas? Do you have any other peanut butter treats you especially like?

A PEANUT BUTTER POLL

How about a peanut butter class survey? Collect the information on a form like the one shown. Then use it as an article for your school newspaper or as a composition for a class assignment.

Remember this: The year 1990 will be the 100th birthday year of peanut butter. It seems right to have a big celebration for that. Give it some thought. It's never too early to plan a centennial celebration.

NAME	FAVORITE PLAIN	FAVORITE CHUNKY	FAVORITE SANDWICH	OTHER SNACK
JILL		✓	WITH JELLY	COOKIES
ROBERT		✓	WITH HONEY	
HORACE	✓		WITH BANANAS	
AMBER		✓		

Is There Butter in Your House?

Which is mostly used in your house, butter or margarine? Can you tell the difference? Have you ever tried?

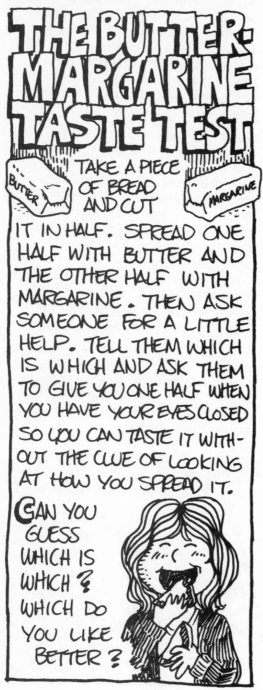

THE BUTTER-MARGARINE TASTE TEST

TAKE A PIECE OF BREAD AND CUT IT IN HALF. SPREAD ONE HALF WITH BUTTER AND THE OTHER HALF WITH MARGARINE. THEN ASK SOMEONE FOR A LITTLE HELP. TELL THEM WHICH IS WHICH AND ASK THEM TO GIVE YOU ONE HALF WHEN YOU HAVE YOUR EYES CLOSED SO YOU CAN TASTE IT WITHOUT THE CLUE OF LOOKING AT HOW YOU SPREAD IT.

CAN YOU GUESS WHICH IS WHICH? WHICH DO YOU LIKE BETTER?

Today people buy more than twice as much margarine as they do butter. One reason is the price. Margarine is cheaper to buy. Some people think that margarine is less fattening than butter, but that's not so. They both provide the same number of Calories.

Take a poll of the grownups in your life. Ask them: (1) Which do you mostly use, butter or margarine? (2) Why? See what conclusions you can make.

I USE MARGARINE BECAUSE BUTTER HAS CHOLESTEROL.

I USE BUTTER OF COURSE... WHO EVER HEARD OF CRAB LEGS DIPPED IN MARGARINE SAUCE?

People have been making butter for a long time, but they didn't always eat it. Greeks and Romans used it just as a medicine. They put it on burns. Some people still do this when they burn themselves, but doctors agree that it's not a good idea at all. Cold water is the best thing to put on a burn, and if you go to the doctor all smeared with butter, it will only have to be washed off — which hurts.

In Spain, up to 300 years ago, people did eat it. But still only as a medicine.

BEAT YOUR OWN BUTTER!

It's not hard to make butter. You can try it yourself. What you need are the following:

    ½ pint of heavy or whipping cream
    a bowl
    an eggbeater
    a wire strainer
    a quart of ice water waiting in the refrigerator

Leave the cream out of the refrigerator for at least an hour while the water is getting cold inside. If the cream is at room temperature, it will turn to butter faster.

Then pour the cream into the bowl and beat it with the eggbeater. Beat hard and keep beating. Maybe you should invite a friend over for some muscle help when you try this. It will take about ten minutes before little globs of fat will begin sticking to the beater. Keep beating.

You're almost there now. When no more butter collects on the insides of the beaters, you've done that part.

There will be some liquid left in the bowl. That's buttermilk. Pour it through the wire strainer into a glass. Put the glass in the refrigerator to chill. It's a good drink.

There will probably be a little butter left in the wire strainer now. Scrape the butter off the beater and put it into the wire strainer too. Pour that quart of ice water over the butter. That will wash off any extra buttermilk.

Put the butter in a bowl. Use the back of a spoon and squish the butter up onto the sides of the bowl. That will get any determined drops of buttermilk to the bottom of the bowl. Pour those out too. You'll have a little more than a quarter pound of butter when you're through.

Most butter sold is salted. You can salt yours by adding ¼ teaspoon of salt and mixing it well.

It's ready to eat now. Spread it on a piece of bread and munch away.

People used to make their own butter. They'd take the cream off the top of milk containers and make butter from it in wooden churns. Kids were expected to help churn. It takes the cream from nine quarts of cow's milk to make a pound of butter.

What color is the butter you made? Compare it to the color of the butter you buy. Today, most butter has yellow food coloring added. That's okay according to government regulations, and it's not necessary to list it on the package.

It used to be that "summer butter" was much more yellow than butter made in the winter. In the summer cows can eat fresh grass, and fresh grass if full of carotene, a substance that has a yellow color. Not all cows today get the chance to munch on fresh grass; color is added to butter so it looks the same all year.

The Other Spread

Margarine was invented as a butter substitute. A chemist did it. His name was Hypolite Mege-Mouries. He lived in France, and in 1867, Napolean III came to him and said he'd reward him with a wonderful prize if he could find a way to make cheap butter for the army, the navy, and poor people.

He did it. He made a pearly white substitute. He used suet, which is fat from animal kidneys. He named this new product *margarites* after the Greek word meaning pearly.

Other methods of making margarine were explored. Today it's made from various oils, including soybean oil, corn oil, and peanut oil.

There was a time when margarine could not be colored before it was sold. You had to buy it white with a capsule of coloring you could mix in yourself, if you wanted to. Check with older people in your family, and ask them if they can remember that.

When margarine is made today, vitamin A is added to make it as nutritious as butter. Both butter and margarine are energy foods, as well as vitamin A sources. You should have one or the other in your diet every day.

Is Chewing Gum a Food?

Yes, chewing gum is a food. It's another development of the food industry, but it doesn't do much for you nutritionally, aside from providing some energy value.

Some people say that gum chewing has some other benefits, though. It helps on airplanes when your ears get clogged and need to pop. The rhythm of chewing helps some people to stay calm. It gets your saliva flowing, and that's a help for digestion.

The Pilgrims learned to chew it from the Native Americans. What they chewed then wasn't what you buy today. It was the resin from the black spruce tree.

In 1850 John Bacon Curtis, who lived in Maine, decided to manufacture that gum and sell it. He took gum from the spruce tree and cooked and stirred it until it thickened. Then he rolled it into a slab, a quarter of an inch thick. He cut it into small pieces about one-half inch by three-fourths of an inch, dipped each piece in cornstarch, and wrapped it in tissue. It was called the State of Maine Pure Spruce Gum, and pieces sold two for a penny. John Curtis's son, John, Jr., went out to sell it. And they sold a lot of gum.

The first bubble gum was invented later, in 1906, by Frank Fleer. Imagine all the chewing he did before he found the right mix. It was called Blibber-Blubber. But it was too sticky. If you blew a bubble, and it broke, it was a dreadful mess to peel off your face and nose. It wasn't until 1928 that this problem was partially solved with the invention of Dubble Bubble by Walter Diemer.

The Japanese manufacture over 150 flavors of gum, including pickled plum. How do you think you would like that? Americans are big chewers too. If all the gum that Americans chewed in one year was made into one stick, it would reach to the moon and back about six times. That's a lot of chewing.

A Chef Invents the Potato Chip

Potato chips are the largest selling snack food in the United States. That invention was made in 1853.

George Crumb was a chef. He worked at Moon's Lake House, a vacation place in Saratoga Springs, New York.

One night George Crumb was cooking as usual. A waiter brought back a man's dinner plate with a complaint. He said

that the fried potatoes weren't thin enough. George Crumb took pride in his work and fixed another batch. The waiter came back again — not thin enough. George Crumb tried again. Still, they came back.

He had enough of this. He sliced some potatoes as thin as he possibly could. They were as thin as the paper this story is written on. He fried them up in boiling fat, and not very cheerfully, sent them out on the plate.

There's a happy ending though. The customer loved them. They were so thin, so crisp, and so delicious that news of them began to spread.

Millions of people have eaten them since. Today about 15 percent of all the potatoes used in the United States wind up as chips.

It's been figured that one person eats about ten pounds of potato chips a year. Do you?

Most of these foods have been invented as convenience foods. And people must want them, since they fill up the supermarket shelves and sell. Over half of what's on those supermarket shelves has been invented in the last 25 years or so, mostly by scientists who work for the food companies.

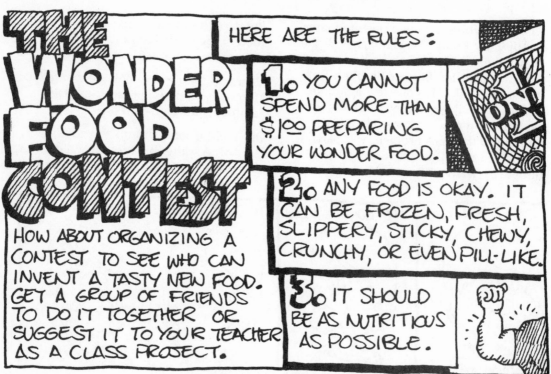

THE WONDER FOOD CONTEST

HOW ABOUT ORGANIZING A CONTEST TO SEE WHO CAN INVENT A TASTY NEW FOOD. GET A GROUP OF FRIENDS TO DO IT TOGETHER OR SUGGEST IT TO YOUR TEACHER AS A CLASS PROJECT.

HERE ARE THE RULES:

1. YOU CANNOT SPEND MORE THAN $1.00 PREPARING YOUR WONDER FOOD.

2. ANY FOOD IS OKAY. IT CAN BE FROZEN, FRESH, SLIPPERY, STICKY, CHEWY, CRUNCHY, OR EVEN PILL-LIKE.

3. IT SHOULD BE AS NUTRITIOUS AS POSSIBLE.

Here's an example of what you might invent. This is a yummy snack that will also add some protein to your daily diet. Mix half a cup of peanut butter with about three soup spoons of nonfat dry milk. Add a spoon or two of honey, if you want to sweeten it. Mix this together so it's pretty stiff and not too sticky. Adding a little more dry milk will help unstick it. Then add half a cup of raisins. Mix them in with your hands. Roll the mixture into a log about one inch thick. Chill it. Then it's ready to slice into bite-sized pieces to eat.

Now if you wanted that snack to be an entry in the wonder food contest, it would need a little help. A long log of peanut butter and raisins doesn't do much for the imagination. It sounds just a bit boring. How about rolling the mixture into individual snacks? Maybe into different letters of the alphabet so people can eat their own initials. Remember, packaging is an important part of the success of foods these days.

Now you need a name for it. Something clever, easy to say, so people will remember it. How about Alphasnacks? Or Nutty Letters? Got the idea?

You'll need a committee of tasting judges to pick a winner. School counselors, brothers and sisters, school bus drivers, parents, grandmothers all make good judges. Put together a committee for this.

You'll need to make scoring sheets for the judges. Here's a sample. Judges have to circle a score in each category and add up the total.

JUDGE _____

FOOD ENTERED BY _____

NAME OF FOOD _____

INGREDIENTS _____
_____
_____

LOOKS

POOR   GREAT

1   2   3   4   5   6

TASTE

POOR   GREAT

1   2   3   4   5   6

NUTRITIONAL QUALITY

POOR   GREAT

1   2   3   4   5   6

TOTAL SCORE: _____

Pick a date for all the foods to be judged. Make a celebration out of it too. Before the judges taste, each person gets to introduce their food. They get to tell how it's nutritious and why it's tasty. They get to use their clever name. Maybe have a testimonial from a friend, and don't forget advertising. That's what helps to make those new products sell.

21
The Ice Cream Story

The ice cream story is a long one. It wasn't a one night discovery like George Crumb's potato chips. New ice cream developments have been made over the past 2,000 years.

Some say it was the Romans who ate the first ice cream. The Roman emperors liked to serve iced desserts for dinner. In order to do this, they had to have slave runners relay snow and ice from the Alps to Rome. That was quite a trek. It meant that the emperors had to plan their menus about a month ahead. That's a lot more fuss than opening the freezer compartment of your refrigerator.

Marco Polo was an Italian explorer. He added to the ice cream story. In the second half of the thirteenth century, he returned to Italy from the Orient. One of the things he brought back was a sherbet recipe. That was a big hit and soon spread throughout Italy.

Kings and Queens
Get the Ice Cream Fever

Ice cream spread farther than Italy too. In the sixteenth century, Catherine de Medici of Italy married Henry II of France, so she moved to Paris with her ice cream makers (as well as other things too). Her son loved ice cream so much that he ate some every day. But the general public never tasted it. The secret of making ice cream was kept carefully guarded.

King Charles I of England had a chef who made yummy ice cream. Charles liked it so much that he declared the recipe a royal secret. That was 1640. He paid his cook a yearly salary for life to keep the secret.

This secret keeping by the royalty just didn't work though. History marched on and so did ice cream.

Public ice cream shops began to open. Italians get the credit for opening the first one, but that happened in Paris in 1660. The ice cream shops spread to the United States too. Philip Lenzi opened the first American ice cream shop in New York City in 1774. He made ice cream mainly on special order. But by 1777, he had ice cream available almost every day.

The Presidents
Get the Taste

George Washington was a known ice cream lover. He owned two ice cream makers, then called ice cream pots. They were made of pewter. In the summer of 1790, he spent $200 on ice cream. At that time, $200 bought a lot more than it does today. He must have eaten quite a pile of ice cream.

Thomas Jefferson liked ice cream so much that he brought a recipe back from France that took 18 different operations to make. He also liked his ice cream best when it was served in a warm pie crust.

Alexander Hamilton's wife made ice cream. Once, at a special dinner, she served an ice cream dessert that was colored red and white.

Dolly Madison was the wife of the fourth president of the United States. She was known for her terrific ice cream desserts. One special treat was the strawberry ice cream she served to the guests at the 1812 Inaugural Ball.

Here's an old recipe for ice cream. It was in a book called *The Italian Confectioner* that was published in 1861.

Whip a pint of fresh double cream, quite strong; when whipped, add to it six ounces of sugar; put it into freezing-pot, and work it well.

Sound easy enough? Well it's the freezing pot part that takes the muscle. The cream and sugar mix is in a container. And that container is submerged in a larger container, with room around it to put ice and salt. The cream mixture gets stirred, and it gets thicker and thicker until it freezes into ice cream.

AS THE ICE CREAM GETS THICKER, THE TURNING GETS HARDER!

Why salt and ice? If you live where it snows in the winter, you may know that salt is often used on roads to melt the ice so cars can drive more safely. If salt is used to *melt* ice, then why is it used to *freeze* ice cream?

Here's the explanation. When ice melts, it absorbs some heat, and that makes its temperature rise. Salt will help ice melt faster. And when it melts faster, it absorbs heat faster — the heat from the ice cream you want to freeze. The faster it absorbs heat from the cream mixture, the faster the cream becomes ice cream.

But while the salt is melting, the cream mixture needs to be constantly stirred. This adds air to keep it light and smooth. That's where the muscle comes in. As the cream starts to freeze, it gets thicker and thicker and harder to stir. If too much salt is used the cream freezes faster, but the quality won't be as good. And if too little salt is used, then the cream won't freeze fast enough. You'll get butter, not ice cream.

IF YOU CRANK TOO LONG YOU MAY GET BUTTER...

I'VE HEARD OF BUTTER BRICKLE BUT THIS IS RIDICULOUS!

1846: A Big Year for Ice Cream

In 1846 Nancy Johnson invented the home ice cream freezer, small enough for a family to use. The ice cream mix was put in a container, which was submerged in a bucket that held the ice and salt. There was a hand crank that was attached to paddles. When the crank was turned, the paddles mixed the cream. People took turns cranking. When the crank got too hard for anyone to turn, the ice cream was ready.

That same type of ice cream freezer is still used today. Do you know anyone who has one? Ask around, and then see if you can talk them into letting you help make a batch. There are electric ice cream makers available now that do the cranking for you. Some people think that's lots easier.

It usually takes about 20 minutes of cranking to turn the cream mixture into ice cream. Imagine the ice cream manufacturer who made 300 gallons for a Fourth of July celebration in 1890 — all by hand!

The ice cream soda didn't appear until about 1880. There are several different stories about its birth. One goes like this. A popular drink at that time was some fruit syrup, carbonated water, and a little cream. Fred Sanders sold these in Detroit. One day his cream got sour, so he slipped in some vanilla ice cream instead. That was the start of the ice cream soda. It wasn't really invented. It just kind of happened.

It was only one short step, and about ten long years, until the ice cream sundae appeared. That happened in Evanston, Illinois, where ice cream sodas were already a favorite drink. But there was a town law that banned "stimulating beverages" on Sundays, the Sabbath, and that included the fizzy ice cream sodas. So on Sundays, a drugstore operator began to serve ice cream with syrup on it, instead of sodas. He purposely misspelled it *sundae* so as not to get any lawmakers or concerned citizens upset.

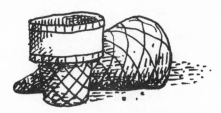

The Ice Cream Cone Breakthrough

It was a hot day in 1904 at the busy St. Louis World's Fair. People were lined up at the ice cream stand, waiting to be served their five or ten cent dishes of ice cream. Then a disaster happened. The ice cream vendor ran out of dishes.

That made the waiting customers very unhappy, and it made the ice cream vendor unhappy too.

The man at the stand next to the ice cream seller noticed this miserable situation. He was selling a kind of Persian waffle. When he noticed the situation, he rolled one of his waffles into a cone and gave it to the ice cream vendor as a substitute for a dish. The customers who were waiting all wanted one of those for sure. That did it. The ice cream cone was on its way. By 1924 Americans were eating 245 million ice cream cones every year.

The Eskimo Pie was an invention made in 1919. A boy in Christian Nelson's store in Iowa couldn't make up his mind whether he wanted ice cream or a candy bar. Mr. Nelson had a nifty idea. Why not have both in one. It was a good idea. In 1921 he started to sell these chocolate-covered ice cream bars, without sticks, and he called them Eskimo Pies. A year later the company was selling a million a day. Now, about 750 million are being sold each year in six different countries.

Tom Carvel invented a soft ice cream machine in 1939. He sold soft ice cream from trucks and stands. It caught on as an ice cream treat that is still available.

Today in San Francisco, you can buy an ice cream treat that you can't get anywhere except near San Francisco. It's called an It's It, and was invented in 1928. If you ever get to San Francisco, race to the nearest market to get one. It is two very big oatmeal cookies with vanilla ice cream between them, all dipped in chocolate. You'll know It's It when you eat one.

The Ice Cream Industry Today

The ice cream industry is a big and busy business today. Almost 8 percent of all milk produced in the United States is used by the ice cream makers. What's in the ice cream you buy in the supermarket today varies a great deal from the way ice cream was first made. The brands of ice cream available vary from each other too.

The Food and Drug Administration has set some standards for ice cream. This was done in 1966. The ice cream sold in markets must be at least 10 percent butterfat. (Regular whipping cream is more than twice that rich.) It can be pumped with air so its volume doubles, but a gallon of ice cream must weigh at least four and a half pounds.

Ice cream can be artificially flavored. If a container of ice cream says vanilla ice cream, then it is flavored with natural flavors. If it says vanilla-flavored ice cream, then it has some artificial flavoring in it, but more natural is used. But if it says artificial or artificially flavored vanilla ice cream, then it uses more artificial flavoring.

Some people say this is fine, ice cream still tastes good. Some people say that it's a shame; ice cream today is nothing like the ice cream made from fresh, rich ingredients. Still, Americans eat a lot of ice cream — about 700 million gallons each year.

THE FLAVORS IT COMES IN

HOW MANY ICE CREAM FLAVORS CAN YOU REMEMBER IF YOU TRY?

IT'S A GOOD IDEA TO TRY REMEMBERING WITH SOME FRIENDS. ONE WAY TO DO THIS IS TO TAKE TURNS, EACH PERSON NAMING AN ICE CREAM FLAVOR THAT HASN'T BEEN MENTIONED BEFORE. SEE HOW LONG YOUR GROUP CAN GO BEFORE YOU RUN OUT. HAVE SOMEONE KEEP COUNT, JUST TO SEE HOW LONG A LIST YOU CAN COME UP WITH.

THE ICE CREAM QUIZ

THE ANSWERS:

Try answering these questions to see what you know about ice cream. Then check your answers. And then try out the quiz on someone else to test their Ice Cream I.Q.

1. What's the favorite ice cream flavor in the U. S. today?

2. What's the second favorite flavor?

3. In which state is the most ice cream eaten per person?

4. What's the favorite flavor in Texas?

5. How many quarts of ice cream on an average does a person eat in a year?

6. How much ice cream was in the biggest ice cream sundae ever made?

7. What ice cream flavor was the biggest flop in history?

8. At what temperature is ice cream best served?

9. If an ice cream store sells 31 flavors, how many different possible double-dip ice cream cones are there?

10. What's a Baked Alaska?

1. Vanilla. About 51 percent of all ice cream sales is vanilla.

2. Chocolate is second and accounts for 13.5 percent of all ice cream sales. Strawberry comes in third at 6 percent.

3. Alaskans eat the most ice cream. They eat about six gallons a year per person.

4. Texans like pecan ice cream.

5. Fifteen quarts a year for an average person.

6. The biggest ice cream sundae ever made used 777 gallons of ice cream. It was made in Virginia in front of a crowd of thousands. There were over two million Calories in that sundae!

7. Chile con carne. Americans had more sense than to buy that one.

8. Ice cream should be 12 degrees F when served. Your freezer is about 0 degrees F, so ice cream should soften a bit before you eat it. You just spend your time mushing it up in the bowl anyway.

9. A lot. Exactly 496 combinations.

10. A Baked Alaska is an ice cream treat, actually baked in the oven. It's ice cream piled on cake, covered with a topping of egg whites beaten with sugar, and baked in the oven. Check a cookbook to try it.

22

Are There Unhealthy Foods?

There are many people who have become very, very concerned about all the packaged, canned, and frozen foods in the supermarket. They feel that when food manufacturers process foods in some way, nothing good happens. In fact, they feel, lots bad can.

For example, these people feel that there are real differences between eating fresh fruit salad and eating canned fruit cocktail. Taste, for one. Nutritional value, for another.

Whenever food is processed, changes are made. Additives and preservatives are usually put in. Let's look at ice cream again. Most ice cream sold in supermarkets has several chemical additions: stabilizers to keep it smooth, emulsifiers so it freezes better, antioxidants to keep it from spoiling, surfactants to keep it moist and firm, artificial dyes for color. There has been concern about how healthy all those chemicals are.

Maybe you've read or heard about organic foods, natural foods, and health foods. Some of these are different foods than what's usually sold in supermarkets.

Natural Foods

Natural foods are foods that haven't been changed in any way before you buy them. You may fix them at home, but they're not processed, not refined, and have nothing added and nothing beneficial removed. It's the difference between fresh fruit salad and canned fruit cocktail, between homemade chicken soup and a package of soup mix you add water to. It's important to weigh the convenience you get from a TV dinner with its additives against the job of fixing your own and knowing you're getting really good food because you're deciding what goes into it.

Organic Foods

Then there are people who say, sure natural foods are better than processed foods, but that's not enough. Most of the fresh foods you buy in the stores have been grown with chemical pesticides to protect them, and those pesticides get passed on to you when you

eat them. Most animals are fed chemical growth stimulants to get them to the market faster and fatter. These people feel it's not good to eat meat with those chemicals in it.

They say it's best to eat only *organic* foods. Organic foods include vegetables grown with natural fertilizers and with no chemicals used. It's possible to buy foods that meet these requirements, but they're not in great supply. And they're usually sold in stores that specialize in organic foods.

Health Foods

There are also *health* foods. These are the kinds of foods which some people think have extra nutritional value and should be added to your diet. You usually don't find these products on your supermarket shelves. They're sold in health food stores. If you're interested, visit a health food store and talk with the person there to learn some more.

What are you going to do with all this information? You'll find some people who think that there's no such thing as an unhealthy food, and they say you should eat whatever you find. Others are sure this isn't so; they believe you need to make your food choices more carefully — lots more carefully. It isn't easy to know what to believe. It's a question of *you* deciding what you think.

23
Learning to Read Labels

One way to get a hint about what you're actually eating when you open a can of food is to read the label. Whenever food manufacturers process and package food, they're required to have certain information on the labels. That's a requirement set by federal law.

Go get a can of soup or some other food from the kitchen cupboard. It will help you to learn about the label information that's required. It's not hard, once you take a look.

Got the can? Then you're set.

Read each requirement below and try to find it on the can you've got. If there are any you can't find, ask someone else to help. It's there somewhere.

The Basic Information on Every Label

First, the name of the product, like cream of mushroom soup or green beans or cling peaches.

Second, the variety, style, and packing medium. That's information like "con-densed" soup or "French style" green beans or peaches packed in "heavy syrup."

Next, the weight of what's in it, not including the can or jar or package. That's listed as net weight.

Last, the name, city, state, and zip code of the manufacturer, packer, or distributor. That's where you should write if you've got any questions about the product.

Information Sometimes on Labels

This information only has to be on labels if it applies to the product.

One is the list of any special diet characteristics, such as "salt free" or "enriched" or "artificially sweetened." Does your can have any of these?

Also in this category is any indication if the product is different from government regulations. And if so, the label would say either "imitation" or "below standard of quality."

The Ingredients Information

Most foods have to have a list of all the ingredients used in the package. What was used most must be listed first, and the second, next, and so on. Read the list on the can you picked.

This requirement has an extra twist though. There are some foods that don't have to list every ingredient. That's because the government has already stated exactly what has to be in the recipe for that product. Once that's set by law, the label only has to list any ingredients that are extra, that aren't in the government recipe.

There are hundreds of these recipes. They all fall into one of these categories: cocoa products, flour, macaroni and noodle products, breads and rolls, milk and cream products, cheese and cheese products, frozen desserts, food flavorings, salad dressings, canned fruit and fruit juices, fruit pies, jellies and jams, canned vegetables, nonalcoholic beverages, oleomargarine, nut products, tomato products.

This makes it tricky for you to know the ingredients, since you don't have the of-

ficial government recipe book. The recipes appear in what's called Title 21, Code of Federal Regulations. It's a complicated document. There are 40 pages just on frozen desserts, 44 pages on canned fruits and juices, 17 pages on canned vegetables. If you want to know about a particular food you eat a lot of, like some jam or jelly, you can write to the Food and Drug Administration, Washington, D. C. 20204, and tell them what you'd like to know. They can help you get the part of the code you need.

The Nutritional Information

This is required only on certain products, those that are "enriched," "fortified," or make any mention of protein, fat, calories, or other special dietary uses on the package. But even though it's not required for all foods, many have that information on the label anyway.

Here's what must be included by law when nutritional information is required:

1. The size of one serving.

2. How many servings in the whole can or container.

3. How many Calories in each serving.

4. How much protein, carbohydrates, and fats in grams, per serving.

5. What percent of your recommended daily allowance is supplied in each serv-

ing for protein, vitamin A, thiamin, riboflavin, niacin, vitamin C, calcium, and iron.

This is all to help you decide how much food value you get from the product you buy. What is on the can you're looking at?

There are still things you don't know. When was this can made? How long was it on the supermarket shelf? How long will it stay there before it's removed if no one buys it? How long will this product last, anyway?

How do you feel about that can you just looked at? Pretty nutritious? Read some labels on other foods in the kitchen. Look at some frozen food packages or a bag of potato chips or another snack.

DOES ANYONE YOU KNOW COOK LIKE THIS?

Try this quiz. Here are ingredients copied from various food products. Ask other people in your family to read them too. Try to guess what food each of these made, and imagine someone actually cooking like that.

1. Water, corn syrup, shortening, sugar, whey solids, food starch-modified, dextrose, sodium caseinate, flavoring, gelatin, whole milk solids, monosodium and diglycerides, salt, vinegar, polysorbate No. 60, vanilla, monosodium phosphate, guar gum, lecithin, artificial color, in a crust of wheat flour, sugar, shortening, water, dextrose, graham flour, sorghum grain flour, salt, sodium bicarbonate, ammonium bicarbonate, artificial flavoring and coloring.

2. Enriched egg noodles, salt, dehydrated chicken and chicken broth solids (BHA, propyl gallate and citric acid added to improve stability), natural flavorings, dried corn syrup, monosodium glutamate, hydrogenated vegetable oil, modified cornstarch, dehydrated onions, wheat starch, chicken fat, starch, potato starch, dehydrated parsley, flavoring and coloring.

3. Carbonated water, sugar, caramel color, phosphoric acid, natural flavorings, caffeine.

4. Beef broth, enriched wheat flour, cooked beef, shortening, water, carrots, dehydrated potatoes, tomatoes, salt, beef fat, modified food starch, peas, dextrose, monosodium glutamate, caramel color, dehydrated onions, hydrolyzed plant protein, lactic acid, spices, dehydrated garlic.

5. Sugar, gelatin, adipic acid (for tartness), sodium citrate (controls acidity), fumaric acid (for tartness), natural and artificial flavors with BHA (a preservative), U. S. certified color.

ANSWERS

Well, what do you think? Here's what these are.

1. Lemon cream pie. Did you see any lemon or cream on that list?

2. Chicken noodle soup in a package.

3. Coca-Cola, and it's 99 percent water and sugar.

4. Frozen beef pot pie.

5. That's a gelatin dessert. Can you guess the flavor from the ingredients? It's orange.

That Extra Stuff on the Labels

Go back and check that list of ingredients for chicken noodle soup. Now take a look in a cookbook and see how it suggests you make chicken noodle soup. What is going on here? What kind of weird cooks do these food manufacturers hire?

There are almost 3,000 different extra ingredients that food manufacturers can add to foods when they are processing them. These additives are put in for different reasons. Some add color. Some add flavor. Some are preservatives used so the food will last a long time. Others affect the texture of what you buy. They keep marshmallows soft and ice cream creamy and make jelly thicken.

The food manufacturers say that without all these extra additives, you wouldn't want to buy the foods they process. And not only would you have to start baking

your own cookies, you'd have no quick snacks to munch on, and you'd need to make your own spaghetti sauce from scratch. Processing of foods was developed for people's convenience, so you can have what you want on your table with the least amount of fuss. But you have to take the additives along with the convenience.

Other people say that this is not such good logic — eating a bunch of strange chemicals that you don't know very much about, just doesn't make sense. Okay, maybe some preservatives make sense. Natural flavorings, like salt, pepper, and spices, sure. But to whip up exotic chemical concoctions for people to eat just to make something a bright color or extra creamy or not lumpy just doesn't seem all that necessary. And it may be dangerous to your health.

This is a serious disagreement, and concerned people who are considered to be food experts argue on both sides.

Listen, the food manufacturers say. How would you feel if you got a yen for a piece of bread and butter for a snack, and when you get the butter dish out, you see a cube of pale, whitish stuff? Imagine spreading white stuff on a piece of bread. Imagine biting in. Who would want to buy it? Or banana ice cream too. Who would want to eat white banana ice cream? Do you think these things would bother you?

But people who are concerned want to know more. Well, what happened to yellow butter? Butter used to be yellow. How come it's not still yellow? Are cows somehow different these days? Do they eat chemicals too? What are you using, anyway, to make butter yellow? And if you used real bananas instead of artificial banana flavoring, banana ice cream would look like banana ice cream without anything extra.

Listen, answer the food manufacturers. We're doing a service for you. Lots of what we add to foods are valuable nutrients — vitamins and minerals. What's wrong with that?

Well, the argument continues, why do you need to do that? Good healthy foods have plenty of vitamins and minerals all by themselves. It's only when you start fiddling around with them, processing them and refining them so much, that there isn't any nutritional value left. Then you have to add artificially made vitamins and minerals. It may be cheaper for you to do it that way, but it doesn't sound best for healthy people.

The food manufacturers go on. How would you like to find greenish oranges at the store? We know greenish oranges can be as ripe and delicious as bright orange ones. We know that oranges only turn orange when the weather gets a little cool. And we know people like oranges to be orange. So when we get green oranges from Texas and Florida, we dye them. That's to make food more pleasant for you.

We make peanut butter that stays creamy without a layer of oil you have to stir every time you open the jar. We make artificial chocolate that tastes more chocolatey than real chocolate, and it's cheaper, too. We make bread that feels squishy and fresh when you buy it, and we make it so it stays that way. We do all this with additives. That's why people like our products more and buy more of them.

The argument continues. But how can you be sure these chemicals are safe to eat? Why take a chance for a little appearance and convenience? So people are used to orange oranges — they could get used to green oranges. It's just habit. You put nitrites in hot dogs and bacon and bologna. There have been some tests

94

to show that nitrites cause cancer. Why keep using them? Since 1955 the number of chemicals used as additives has doubled. What else are you using that isn't safe?

You might try writing a letter to the manufacturers of a food product you have in the house, and ask them about what additives they use and how they know they're safe. Listen to advertisements for processed foods and think about the claims these advertisers make. This all concerns your nutritional health.

Where are the Government Regulations Now?

It's a complicated issue to sort out. The government has to approve of what food manufacturers add to foods. There is a listing that the Food and Drug Administration puts out called the GRAS list. That stands for the Generally Recognized As Safe list.

But some people think that the government isn't careful enough with that list. They think the government should take the responsibility for proving them safe. Some chemicals have been taken off the list because they're unsafe after lots of people have already eaten foods with those chemicals added.

The complicated part is balancing the benefits from an additive and the possible risk. After all, with preservatives,

food can travel long distances without spoiling to get to your kitchen table. That's better than having the danger of contamination of food cause general illness. But maybe it's better not to risk adding some additional substance to food that really may not be good for people to eat.

There is research going on, but the research is slow. For example, cyclamates were used as sweetening in many products. People ate food with cyclamates without a thought, but then research showed that cyclamates cause tumors in rats. Finally cyclamates are no longer allowed to be used in manufacturing food for people, but it took a long time.

MSG is still used in foods. It's monosodium glutamate, and its purpose is to bring out the flavor in food. It was found to be dangerous when used in large quantities. The major infant food manufacturers have stopped using it, but the law still doesn't forbid it. It's still used and sold in stores, but nutritionists recommend that it be used very, very little, if at all.

One reason that research is so slow is that research costs a great deal of money. A jar of jam or jelly may say 100 percent pure. That means it follows the official government recipe. But according

to that recipe, the jam can contain citric acid, pectin, sodium citrate, antioxidant, and antidefoaming agent. Only if it says no preservatives, no artificial color, no artificial flavor, can you be sure it has no added chemicals.

What Can You Eat?

It's safest to rely on labels that clearly state no additives, no preservatives, no chemicals added. Check bread for this, cereals too. And stick with fresh foods whenever possible.

Deciding what to eat isn't easy. It's one of those situations where there are experts on both sides of the issue. Some say it's silly to get all upset, look at all the advantages; there's no real danger from additives, no use going back to the Dark Ages. Others say it's not silly to worry; the danger of additives is real and isn't worth the health risk, no matter how easy they make your life.

And where are you? Which expert will you believe? You have the responsibility for taking charge of what you eat. Lots of times you eat where you don't really have control over what the food is — in restaurants, at friends' houses, even at your own dinner table. You've got eating habits that have been built up for a long time too.

Talk all this over with the other people in your family. Chew it over in your head. Finally, remember that you have to make some decisions for you. And that means you have to be your own expert.

24

How Come They're Called Hot Dogs?

The hot dog is one food that many people are very concerned about, very upset about what's really in them. Yet the hot dog is one of the favorite foods in the United States. Americans eat over 15 billion hot dogs each year.

A hot dog is a sausage. There are over 200 different kinds of sausages sold in the United States. But the hot dog outsells them all. People have been making sausages for a long time, at least back to Roman times and maybe longer. The Germans are the most famous for making and inventing lots of kinds of sausages. It's the German influence that first got hot dogs to this country, but how that happened isn't totally clear.

Some people say that Antoine Feuchtwanter was responsible. He was a sausage vendor who came to the United States, and in 1883 he began to sell frankfurters in St. Louis. Frankfurt is a city in Germany, and what he sold was Frankfurt sausage. The story says that when you bought a hot frank from Mr. Feuchtwanter, he gave you a white cotton glove to hold it with.

Other people say that frankfurters first began to be sold at the Chicago World's Fair in 1893 at a German exhibit. The customers weren't returning the white gloves they were loaned, so someone thought to wrap the franks in a bun to eat.

Other people say no, it wasn't that way at all. Charles Feltman lived in New York. He made a visit back to Germany where he was born, and he brought back the frankfurter. Right after 1900, he opened a place to sell them on Coney Island. Nathan Handwerker worked for Mr. Feltman, but in 1916 he opened his own

97

place, called Nathan's Famous, Inc. Nathan's is still going strong and calls itself the greatest hot dog seller in the world.

The name *hot dog* was first used in 1906. Everyone agrees about this part of the hot dog story. A cartoonist called Tad drew a cartoon of a frankfurter with a tail, legs, and a head, so it looked like a strange dachshund. That did it. The name hot dog has been used ever since, and it has spread to other countries too. It's become so well known that some people think hot dogs were an American invention.

Making hot dogs is a complicated process. First the meat used is ground. Then curing ingredients and spices are added. These give flavor, color, and also preserve the hot dogs. This meat mixture is chopped for 8 to 12 minutes, with cold water and ice cubes added to keep it moist and cool. Then the mixture is stuffed into the casings that give hot dogs their shape. After that, the frankfurters are smoked for one to three hours to develop the flavor and color and to destroy any bacteria. Then they're cooked in a giant chamber by being sprayed with hot water. And finally they are chilled with cold water, peeled — so you don't have to do that before you eat them — and packed.

What's Inside?

What actually does go into hot dogs is controlled by United States Department of Agriculture regulations, which are very specific. Hot dogs may be made from just beef or a mixture of beef, pork, and veal, with no more than 30 percent fat. Hot dogs can have up to 10 percent water as well as 2 percent corn syrup and 3.5 percent salt, spices, and curing ingredients. Up to 3.5 percent cereals and non-fat dry milk can be added too. And up to 15 percent poultry can be added. So it's okay for a hot dog to be just a little more than half meat.

This ruling was made in 1969. Before that, the only regulation was that hot dogs should be made of beef, mutton, pork, or goat meat along with fat and no more than 3.3 percent cereal or other filler. Back in the 1930s, hot dogs had about 18 percent fat. But by 1969, the fat averaged 33 percent, and some franks had as much as 51 percent fat.

There was no way for the consumer to know how much fat there was in the hot dogs they bought, and many people thought they were getting protein-packed meat. What people got were often more like fatfurters than frankfurters.

The Hot Dog Arguments

The issue came up in 1969, and lots of people got in on the discussion: the Agriculture Department representatives, concerned consumer groups, meat cutters' and butchers' representatives. They argued about percentages. Finally the argument was over. The 30-percenters had won. Starting in October of 1969, hot dogs and all other federally inspected cooked sausage, like bologna and knockwurst, could have no more than 30 percent fat.

Then another hot dog argument came up — the chicken argument. Chicken growers thought that it should be okay to put chicken in hot dogs along with the meat. Meat producers said no. The compromise for that argument: 15 percent of hot dogs could be chicken, but the label has to say that there is chicken in the hot dogs.

Still another hot dog argument, one that hasn't been resolved yet. Hot dogs are made with various additives. One of these is sodium nitrite, which is added to prevent botulism from growing. Some people are worried because nitrite may be a dangerous substance. It reacts with other chemicals in the food you eat and has been shown to cause cancer in animals. Not only is nitrite used in hot dogs, it's used in all cured meats like bologna, salami, corned beef. The worst of all is bacon.

99

Hot dogs also contain sodium nitrate, which gives the meat that reddish color. And nitrates are also suspected with nitrites of causing cancer. U. S. Department of Agriculture chemists are studying this, but no new regulations have been made yet.

It's not necessary to make hot dogs with nitrites. Some stores sell nitrite-free hot dogs, bologna, and imitation bacon. It's a good idea to check the labels.

Why all the fuss? People have been concerned that hot dogs have become less and less nutritious. Even with no more than 30 percent fat allowed, a hot dog may be only half meat. And hot dogs can legally include parts of animals' bodies you don't usually eat, like the esophagus, diaphragm, and heart, including fat, bone, skin, nerve, and blood vessels. The hot dog industry asked in 1973 to be able to include lips, snouts, and ears too. The regulations don't permit that. Yet.

A hot dog is only 14 percent protein. One frankfurter provides 7 grams of protein. A hamburger that weighs the same provides twice that much. With the added risk of nitrites and nitrates, the hot dog might be a risky chew. It's something to think about the next time you make a hot dog choice.

25
The Breakfast Cereal Business

The breakfast cereal aisle in the supermarket is as dazzling as a used car lot, but there has been a lot of concern about what's in those cereal boxes.

That aisle is a good place to practice your label-reading skills. Then you can decide for yourself how you feel about the breakfast cereals stacked there.

First some history about how breakfast cereals got started. Back in the late 1800s, there was a place where people went for health cures of different types. It was the Battle Creek Sanitorium, run by Dr. John Harvey Kellogg. Most of his cures had to do with fiddling around with patients' diets. Some of them were strange cures. For example, people who were too skinny were fed 26 times a day. They did nothing but stay in bed so they wouldn't use up any extra Calories. They weren't even allowed to brush their teeth because that might use up a few!

One of the theories Dr. Kellogg had was that you needed to chew dry, brittle food to keep your teeth in good shape. But a woman patient broke a tooth on what she was given to chew because it was so hard. So Dr. Kellogg figured out something else for this woman to eat.

What he did was to create a breakfast cereal made from thin flakes of corn. He named them Kellogg's Toasted Corn Flakes. He began to sell them, and they were a huge success.

Charles Post was another patient. He had an ulcer. And though he wasn't cured of that, he did learn something while he was there. He learned that he could get rich from selling a breakfast cereal. So he invented one, too, and named it Elijah's Manna. But he realized it would never sell with that name, so he changed it to Grape Nuts. It didn't have any grapes in it or any nuts, either. It still doesn't. But it was a success. And he went on to create Post Toasties, having learned that a catchy name means a lot.

Today the breakfast cereal business is enormous. And Kellogg's Toasted Corn Flakes is still the biggest seller of all American dry breakfast cereals.

One of the reasons that Americans have taken to breakfast cereals is that they're quick and easy. Instead of having to fuss and cook eggs or bacon or pancakes, all you do is add milk and eat. And people have been told through advertising that they're healthy. Just read on the side of the box about the nutritional value.

Besides, kids like them. They've been specially designed so kids will like them. They come in different shapes, different colors, with different things to read on the boxes as entertainment while you munch. You learn all about this from TV advertising that's directly aimed at you, shown when kids are usually watching.

Just like Dr. Kellogg convinced his patients that it was healthy to lie perfectly still all day, the cereal business had convinced the American public that breakfast cereals are the nutritional answer to that important first meal of the day.

And it's just not so. At least not for all of them on that aisle.

King Vitamin are all more than one-third sugar, some closer to half sugar. A Ding Dong is about 25 percent sugar, and a Mounds candy bar is around 20 percent sugar. Neither would be considered a smart choice to put in a bowl with milk for a nutritious breakfast; yet they have less sugar than those cereals listed. But they're called snacks, and the others are called cereal. And that seems to make a lot of difference about how people think of them.

In August, 1974, there was a big attack on the sugar-coated cereals by nutritionists, dentists, doctors, and other concerned groups. They petitioned the Food and Drug Administration to set some standards for these cereals. They wanted any cereal that had more than 10 percent sugar to state on the package how much it had. They also wanted them to add: "Frequent use contributes to tooth decay and other health problems." The petition was denied, even though one of the head officials of the administration said he wouldn't want his own children to eat that sugared material.

Candy for Breakfast?

Many of the cereals contain more sugar than any other ingredient. Cap'n Crunch, Cocoa Krispies, Alpha Bits, Super Sugar Crisp, Fruity Pebbles, Cocoa Pebbles,

Some nutritionists feel that the sugar-coated cereals don't even have enough cereal in them to count as a breakfast cereal. In 1974 the Food and Nutrition Board, a federal government organization said that sugar-coated cereals should be called and sold as snacks, not as breakfast food. But nothing has been done.

Besides, if you check the prices, you'll find that you pay almost twice as much for the cereal that's sugar-coated as you pay for the same cereal when it's plain. Paying that much more for getting that much less just doesn't make nutritional sense.

More Breakfast Bewares

Besides the sugar problem, some of the cereals sold aren't much more than starch and air: Puffed Wheat and Puffed Rice, for example. Others are sprayed with so many vitamins and minerals, that's about all you get, like Product 19, Concentrate, Kaboom, Total. They're as much vitamin pills as they are breakfast cereals.

Many cereals don't use whole grains. The cereal companies process the whole grains. It's called refining them. And then they have to artificially add nutrients. That's called enriching them. Most nutritionists agree that your body much prefers the natural to the artificial additives.

There have been new "natural" cereals on the supermarket shelves. Even then, you have to be careful. Lots of them have added sugar to the whole grains,

nuts, and seeds in their boxes. Quaker 100% Natural is 20 percent sugar. Maybe they should call it Quaker 80% Natural.

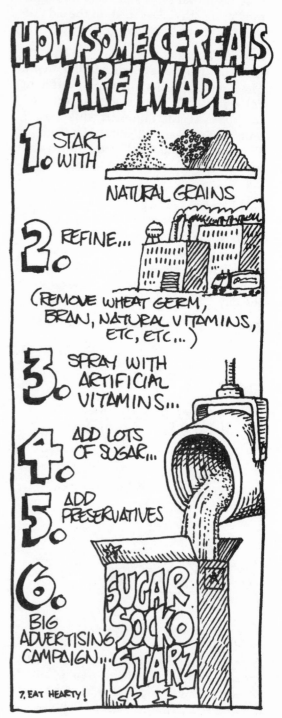

HOW SOME CEREALS ARE MADE

1. START WITH NATURAL GRAINS

2. REFINE... (REMOVE WHEAT GERM, BRAN, NATURAL VITAMINS, ETC, ETC...)

3. SPRAY WITH ARTIFICIAL VITAMINS...

4. ADD LOTS OF SUGAR...

5. ADD PRESERVATIVES

6. BIG ADVERTISING CAMPAIGN... SUGAR SOCKO STARZ

7. EAT HEARTY!

The TV Message

Think of the cereal commercials you've seen on TV. Next time you see one, listen carefully, and see how you are being convinced to want that cereal for breakfast.

Imagine an ad that would tell you what's *really* in the cereal and what it could do for you.

Every time you buy cereal, one-third of the price you pay goes for advertising.

All Cereals Aren't Bad

There are some cereals that aren't overly processed, overly sugared, or sprayed with vitamins, like oatmeal, wheat germ, shredded wheat, some granola-type cereals, Familia, Wheatena, and others.

You need to sharpen your supermarket eye. Next time someone in your family is going to do the shopping, go along. Check out the breakfast cereal aisle. Look at the ingredients listed on the cereal boxes.

How many of them list sugar first? That means that there is more sugar inside that box than anything else. If sugar isn't first, look over the list; see if corn syrup or honey are listed and how far along in the list they are. They're just different forms of the same villain. Sometimes if they were all combined, they'd easily go first.

Here are two actual ingredient listings from two cereal boxes. *Label 1:* 100% toasted wheat. No added preservatives or additives.

In each serving: Calories — 110, Protein — 3 grams, Carbohydrates — 21 grams, Fat — 1 gram.

Label 2: Puffed-Milled Corn, Sugar, Corn Syrup, Molasses, Salt, Hydrogenated Vegetable Oil, Sodium Ascorbate, Vitamin A Palmitate, Niacinamide, Zinc Oxide, Ascorbic Acid, Artificial Coloring, Reduced Iron, Riboflavin (B2), Pyridoxine Hydrochloride (B6), Thiamin Hydrochloride (B1), Folic Acid, Vitamin D2, BHA and BHT added to preserve product freshness.

In each serving: Calories — 110, Protein — 1 gram, Carbohydrates — 26 grams, Fat — 0 grams.

What's wrong with the second label? Even though sugar isn't listed first, it's listed second with two other sweeteners following, corn syrup and molasses. This cereal has been colored with artificial coloring. There are no whole grains in it at all; its base is processed corn.

What's right with the first label? It's made with whole wheat. There's no added sugar. There's not artificial coloring. It provides three times as much protein in a serving as the other cereal.

You don't have to eat a worthless breakfast. The cereal makers seem to be more interested in selling you some breakfast food that is just fortified fluff. Don't fall for it.

26

Is Breakfast Really So Important?

Yes. Breakfast is very, very important.

Suppose you eat supper at 6 p.m. Your digestive system gets to work, and by 9 p.m., the proteins have begun to be absorbed from your small intestine. You may even go to sleep before all the protein gets absorbed. But your food energy is all used up by 6 the next morning.

Now if you rush off to school at 8 a.m. without eating any breakfast, you haven't given your body any more protein. And even if you eat an okay lunch at about noon, the protein from that lunch won't start to get to where it's needed until about 3 p.m.

That means from 6 a.m. until 3 p.m., there is a nine hour protein gap in your body. You may make up for it after school and at supper, but for those nine hours, you are putting some stress on your body.

It's not a great danger. Your body does have a small protein bank account which it draws on when it needs to. But you may not be as sharp as you need to be. Studies have shown that kids who don't eat a good breakfast often have trouble doing as well as they could in school.

That's not necessary. Besides, it's no way to treat the only body you've got.

Your body also needs more than protein. You need carbohydrates and fats for energy. If you don't eat, your body will dip into your reserves, too, to keep those fires burning in your cells. But that's just not as efficient for you as providing the fuel you need by eating.

Is Breakfast a Problem for You?

There are two major anti-breakfast arguments from most breakfast skippers: the "I don't have time in the morning" argument and the "I hate to face food so early" argument. They're toughies. If one of these is yours, you may be one of those breakfast avoiders.

Maybe what you need is a new approach to breakfast. Whoever said that the only food you can eat for breakfast is "breakfast food"? Eggs, toast, juice, cereal, pancakes are what people usually think of as breakfast foods.

Why not think about your breakfast in a new way? Take a peek in the refrigerator, if you get your own breakfast. Maybe there's a piece of cold chicken left from last night's dinner. There's a starter. How about a toasted cheese sandwich? Maybe peanut butter or tuna. Think about nutritious food that you like to eat other times of the day, and think about having those for breakfast. And don't forget to have a glass of milk along with whatever you fix.

Try getting inspiration from other people you know too. Ask around, especially older people like your grandparents. Ask them what they usually ate for breakfast when they were about your age. Collect as many different breakfast menus as you can. Maybe you could write a breakfast cookbook to help others put a little pizzazz into their breakfasts.

If you eat a good breakfast every day, give yourself a pat on your back and keep up the good work. Maybe you could encourage other kids to do the same.

Breakfast wasn't always so routine. There was an Englishman who lived in the United States around 1860. He was a newspaper reporter for the *London Times*. In one article, he reported that an American started the day with a breakfast of "black tea and toast, scrambled eggs, fresh spring shad, wild pigeons, pigs' feet, two robins on toast, and oysters." That sounds like a bit much, but it sure wasn't like breakfast food as you know it today.

The Good-Breakfast Campaign

Here's an idea that you could do as a boost-for-breakfast project. What you need is a good supply of snappy looking buttons that say "I Ate a Good Breakfast Today!" You can make them by cutting shapes out of heavy paper or cardboard and taping a safety pin onto the back. A cheery sunny-side up fried egg is a good shape to start with. Write the message on the yolk.

Wear a button to school one day. Someone is bound to ask you what it is. Tell them, proudly, "I know a good breakfast is important, so I ate one. Did you?" And if they say yes, whip out another button, and pin it right on them. You

might start a breakfast revolution. Suggest this to your teacher as a class project. Give breakfast a boost in the whole school.

27
Do You Really Have to Eat Your Vegetables?

Vegetables are absolutely necessary for good health. They provide proteins and carbohydrates, plus those essential vitamins and minerals. How do you feel about vegetables? Do you get your daily needs met?

There are lots of different vegetables that people eat. You don't need to eat them all, but enough to give you a variety. The vegetables you eat come from different plants and also different parts of those plants. When you eat lettuce or spinach, you're eating the leaves of plants. Broccoli is the flower and the stem of the plant. Peas and corn are the seeds. Tomatoes and cucumbers are the fruits of plants, but you eat them as vegetables. When you eat asparagus, you're eating the stalk. Carrots are roots. White potatoes are tubers, which are little lumps on the roots of the potato plants. You also eat bulbs, like onions.

A VEGETABLE INVESTIGATION!

Get a piece of paper and fold it into eight sections. Label each section with a different part of plants that people eat. Here's what your paper should look like.

Now think about the vegetables you eat. For each vegetable, decide which part of the plant it is. Then write the name of the vegetable in the correct box on your paper. Write the name of any vegetable you don't know on the back of the paper, and check with one of your parents to get some help. Try this now and save your paper. There will be more for you to do with it as you keep reading.

LEAVES	FLOWERS	SEEDS	FRUIT
STALKS 'N' STEMS	ROOTS	TUBERS	BULBS

Why do people eat the vegetables they do and not others? Some plants are poisonous — rhubarb, for instance. Have you ever eaten rhubarb pie? It's tasty. It's made from the stalks of the rhubarb plants, not the leaves. The leaves are poisonous and will make you very sick.

Then there are plenty of other plants people don't eat, because they just don't. Maybe they just don't like the taste of them, or maybe it's just not the custom, and no one has tried it yet.

Zucchini flowers are an example of this for some people. Most people who eat zucchini (do you?) eat the fruit of the plant. It grows at the end of the zucchini blossom, which is a beautiful, big yellowish orange flower. The plant produces some blossoms which don't produce zucchini. And some people eat those blossoms. They stuff them with a tasty bread filling, dip them in a batter, and fry them. Have you ever tasted them?

There may be lots of things people don't eat because they think they're strange and yucky. When the potato was brought to Europe from Peru, where it was first grown, people would have nothing to do with it. How weird to eat that lump

I THINK I'M BEAUTIFUL!!

that grows off the root with its strange parts like eyes, they thought. Yet today, potatoes are an important part of many people's diets.

People in parts of China like to eat raw garlic, big chunks of garlic that have been soaked in soy sauce. Seaweed has been eaten for a long time by Japanese people. It's rich in minerals.

Have you ever eaten an artichoke? Can you imagine the first person who ever tried to do that? It's one of those foods that's okay to eat with your hands at the dinner table — in a very interesting way. Ask your parents, if you don't know about it.

How fussy are you about the vegetables you eat? Go back over that list you made and mark all the ones you really dislike with an X. Mark the ones you like a lot with a check. Put an O next to the ones you eat without complaining, but you're not really crazy about. How does your vegetable picture look? Is your picture like the picture of the other people in your family?

Make a prediction about how your parents or sister or brother would mark them, and then check out your predictions. How well do you know what your family likes to eat?

A VEGETABLE QUIZ

Try answering these questions and see how many you know. Then ask the rest of your family to try them, maybe sometime when you're all eating together.

1. What is the most ancient vegetable still grown today?

2. What's the biggest selling vegetable in the U. S. today?

3. What vegetable do you eat that is related to the morning glory? (Hint: It's often eaten at Thanksgiving.)

4. What vegetable is usually used to make pickles?

5. Name a vegetable that you can eat both the leaves and the roots of.

6. Name all the vegetables that you can think of that are reddish in color, inside or outside or both.

7. What vegetable is a member of the cabbage family and looks like miniature cabbages?

8. When this vegetable was first grown in the U. S., you'd have to take a train to Kalamazoo, Michigan, to get some. What is it?

9. There is a vegetable that is related to the lily. What is it?

10. About how many kernels are on a corncob about eight inches long?

11. How come people sometimes say that someone is "cool as a cucumber"?

12. What kind of vegetable is an "aubergine"?

13. What vegetable is very dangerous to pick wild and eat?

14. Which state in the U. S. grows the most spinach?

15. Which vegetable is sold mostly in October?

A VEGETABLE QUIZ ANSWERS

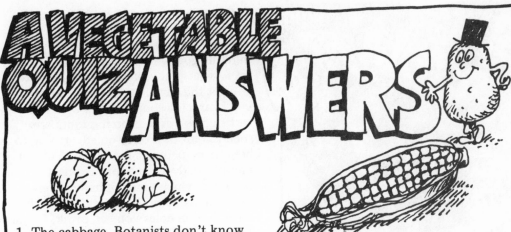

1. The cabbage. Botanists don't know where or when it originated, but it has been cultivated for over 4,000 years. That's probably because it grows almost anywhere.

2. The potato is first, followed by lettuce and tomatoes.

3. It's the sweet potato.

4. Cucumber, usually, though people have been known to pickle all sorts of things, including the rind of watermelons.

5. You can eat the greens and the roots of the beet and turnip. Do you know any others?

6. Some reddish vegetables: beets, red cabbage, red onions, tomatoes, radishes.

7. Brussel sprouts.

8. It's celery.

9. The onion is related to the lily.

10. It varies. Somewhere between 600 and 700, probably.

11. That's because a cucumber really is cool inside, about 20 degrees cooler than the air outside on a warm day.

12. "Aubergine" is the French name for the eggplant. It's used in Great Britain too.

13. Mushrooms. Some mushrooms are highly poisonous and can cause death.

14. Texas.

15. Pumpkins, of course. About 80 percent of all the pumpkins sold each year are sold in October.

How Come No One Advertises Broccoli?

It has been said that kids don't like vegetables. Do you think that's true? Then it has been said that maybe the reason kids don't like vegetables is that no one takes the trouble to fix them so they're as delicious as they could be. Do you think that's true too?

And then some people say that the real reason kids don't like vegetables is because of advertising. Here's how that thinking goes. Most of what you like to eat is what you've gotten used to. Often you get the chance to get used to what you hear a lot about. That's where advertising comes in. The food industry spends a lot of money on advertising to help shape people's food likes. You get plenty of advertising for breakfast cereals, for which kinds of hamburgers you can get at which places, for all the colas and un-colas you can drink, for all the juice drinks you can glug down.

Well, how come no one advertises vegetables? How come they don't let you know how yummy an artichoke can be? Or about that wonderful crunching you can do with carrots or celery. Or the sweet chewiness of yams. You can't blow bubbles with them, but they're good to eat and healthy too. Or why don't they tell you of all the different ways there are to eat a rutabaga? Rutabaga? Why not? Have you ever tried it? You may be missing something you really could like.

28
What's a Vegetarian?

There are some people who do not eat any animal food at all. That includes all meat, poultry, and fish. They are called vegetarians. Some vegetarians will drink milk and eat eggs and cheese, since they are not the meat of animals. Others choose not to eat food that comes from any animal source at all.

Why? For many different reasons. Some people just don't like to eat meat. So they don't and that's that. Some people feel that it just isn't right to kill animals to feed people. They may drink milk or eat eggs and cheese, but animals don't have to be killed for that.

Other people are vegetarians because it is one of the teachings of their religion. Zen Buddhists, Hindus, and Seventh-Day Adventists are three religious groups that eat vegetarian diets.

Another group of vegetarians do it because of their feelings about the food problem in the world. There are many people in the world who do not have enough to eat. Meat is one of the most expensive foods. In order to raise meat, an enormous amount of grain has to be used to feed the animals, and that costs money too. There is a movement of people who feel that we could satisfy our own nutritional needs just as well by eating the grain, instead of feeding it to animals just so we can eat them. That way, food could cost less, and fewer people would go hungry.

Is a Vegetarian Diet Healthy?

Meat is not absolutely necessary for a healthy diet. Eating a vegetarian diet can be a totally sound, well-balanced way to eat. There is plenty of protein in legumes, grains, and nuts. The trick vegetarians have to learn is which of these foods combined will give them the complete protein needed for good nutrition.

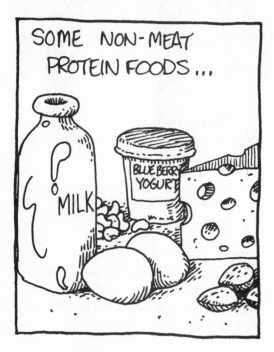

If milk and eggs and cheese are included, there's no worry at all, for they are good protein sources. If milk and eggs and cheese are not included, then there is a problem. A strict vegetarian diet will not provide vitamin B12. Vitamin B12 is found only in animal sources, and it's one of the nutrients every body needs. A vitamin pill is recommended by nutritionists for that problem.

One Person's Wheat Is Another Person's Meat

What do vegetarians eat? Not just vegetables. Vegetarians eat fruits, bread, beans, and other wheat products like noodles, rice, nuts. And they don't just munch on a plate of nuts and vegetables for dinner. There are lots of great ways to fix vegetarian dishes.

There are cookbooks that have been written just giving nifty ideas for vegetarian dishes. And there are restaurants which serve only vegetarian meals. Maybe there's one where you live, and you can ask your parents to take you there so you can try it.

Famous Vegetarians
You May Not Know

Some very famous people were vegetarians. Here's a list of 30 of them. See how many of these famous historical names you recognize.

Plato, Dogenes, Pythagoras, the Buddha, Seneca, Virgil, Ovid, Horace, St. Paul, Plutarch, Shakespeare, Leonardo da Vinci, Newton, Rousseau, Voltaire, Benjamin Franklin, Darwin, Emerson, General William Booth, Thoreau, Shelley, Alexander Pope, Tagore, Tolstoy, H. G. Wells, Edison, Einstein, George Bernard Shaw, Schweitzer, General George Montgomery, Gandhi.

There was a time when people thought that vegetarians were really strange people — food weirdos. After all, what is Thanksgiving without turkey? What kind of crazy wouldn't eat hamburgers? But then there are always people who think that anyone who acts different is strange.

In 1838 there was an American Health Convention, and at that convention, people learned that a vegetarian diet can be a healthy way to eat. Today there are about three million vegetarians in the United States. Maybe you know some. Or maybe you can ask around and see if you can meet someone who has made the choice to be a vegetarian and talk to them about their diet.

29
Vitamins: Your ABC's

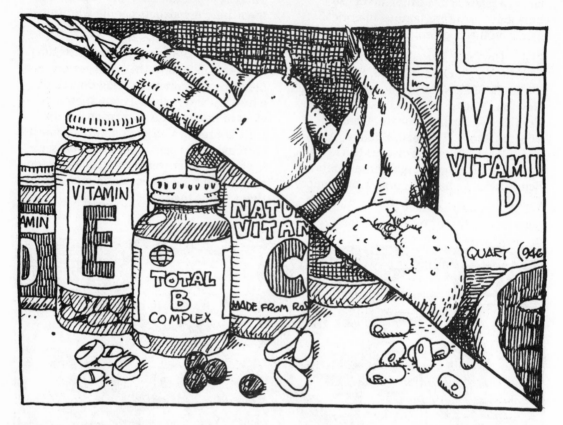

Even though your body is a pretty terrific chemical factory, there are some things it just can't do. One of those things is to manufacture vitamins. Your body needs vitamins, so it's up to you to supply them.

There are 13 vitamins that nutritionists have found your body needs. They can be divided into two groups. One group is called the fat-soluble group. This includes vitamins A, D, E, and K. The other group is the water-soluble vitamins, the B vitamins and vitamin C. The basic difference between these two groups is that your body will store the fat-soluble vitamins when it gets some. But you excrete the water-soluble ones daily.

What actually are vitamins? They are substances found in foods that are needed for your body to function. When your body changes food into energy, it's a complicated chemical process. It couldn't happen without vitamins to help. It's kind of like what happens when you try to open a tightly closed jar. You need two hands. One to hold the jar, one to turn the lid. Vitamins give all the operations carried on in your body that helping hand.

Some examples. When you cut yourself, you often bleed. Pretty soon the bleeding stops because your blood clots. It clots, that is, if you have taken care of your body's need for vitamin K. Your blood won't clot without it.

If you don't get enough vitamin C, you get a disease called scurvy. That was a problem for years among sailors. Often on board ship, there wasn't enough fresh fruit, especially citrus fruits: oranges, grapefruit, lemons, limes. The sailor's gums began to bleed; they got bruised; their bones broke easily. Have you ever heard British sailors called "limeys"? That's because they carried lime juice on board ships to prevent this vitamin problem.

The Vitamin Argument

There's a vitamin argument that's going on among nutritional experts: Should you or shouldn't you take vitamin pills to make sure you're getting what you need?

Some experts say that you get all the nutrients you need from eating a well-balanced diet, and extra vitamins aren't necessary.

Others say that you can't be too sure. Even if you eat a varied, careful diet, many of the foods that you eat have been processed before you buy them, and that often destroys the vitamins. So you may think you're getting what you're not really getting at all.

That's no danger, says the first group. Many foods are fortified with additional vitamins. Most milk has added the vitamin D that you need. Breads are enriched to make sure they provide needed vitamins, and you can read this information on the labels. Also, it's possible to get too many of some vitamins, the fat-soluble ones, and that's not good.

That argument doesn't convince the other group. You shouldn't take chances with your health, they say. A daily vitamin pill won't cause problems of getting too much of any vitamin, and you'll be sure that you're getting what you need.

Then there's still another group which feels that only natural vitamins will do. This group says that if you take vitamin pills, you should check the label very carefully to make sure they are totally natural, not synthetic.

No one really knows for sure. That's because every body is different. What may be good, or enough, for one person, may not be okay for another. There are recommended amounts of vitamins you should get daily. And even those get changed from time to time as nutritionists learn more. Nutritionists haven't known about vitamins long enough for them to have been totally researched yet.

What Should You Do?

Check back to Chapter 8, and make sure your eating is well-balanced. That's the first thing. Vitamins are not substitutes for good eating.

Whether or not to take vitamin pills is a decision you need to make with your parents' help. Check with your doctor or school nurse if you would like to talk with someone else about this issue. But, finally, you'll have to decide which expert to believe. It's your body.

119

30

A Big Problem: Overweight in the U.S.

Have you ever heard grownups talk about going on a diet? Maybe someone in your house has been on a diet, or is on a diet, or is often talking about going on a diet.

Being fat is not healthy. In the past 20 years, more and more has been written about this problem. And more and more people have been talking about it.

There are lots of people in the United States who are too fat. That includes kids too. About one kid out of every five weighs too much. It's gotten to be a national problem.

What do you know about this problem? Are you worried about being fat? Do you know any other kids who are? It's a problem that people can do something about, but it's hard to do alone. Some information can be a help.

Some Solid Facts

Body fat is kind of like raw chicken fat — yellowish and greasy. It's stored in your body in certain cells, and it does some good jobs. Fat helps protect you against cold. It cushions your bones and other organs. Your fat cells are kind of an energy bank for you. When your body needs more fuel than you give it by eating, the fat can be changed into fuel.

But too much fat, that can be a problem. Find a mirror in your house that you can use to see all of you, or as much of you as possible. Take a look. Stand sideways and see if you're pretty flat front to back and top to bottom. Or kind of bulging. Can you see your ribs? Do you look bony or padded?

If your tummy seems round, and your bottom soft, and your face a bit chubby, don't get upset. You may still be in the "baby fat" stage of your life.

What Is Baby Fat?

Think about babies for a minute. Have you noticed how they have bulging bellies and padded arms and legs? Sometimes their wrists are so chubby they look like they have rubber bands on them. About the time that kids start to go to school, they usually lose this layer of fat but not entirely. Some kids don't lose it all until they're full grown.

Look at other kids in your class. Are some taller than others? And thinner? Are some still kind of pudgy? You're all around the same age, and you're not babies, but what's called baby fat may stay around until you start the big growth leap into your adult body. That can start to happen anytime between the ages of 10 and 12. Maybe even older or maybe even younger. Every body is different. Have you noticed that?

**From Baby Fat
to Puppy Fat**

When you start the time of the big growth leap in your life, you can tell. You notice new body hair. You get taller. Your shape starts to change and looks more like an adult shape. And some kids, when that happens, still notice they have extra fat.

Girls usually notice it around their waists, hips, and thighs. Boys on their thighs, abdomens, and nipples. No, it's not baby fat. It's what's called puppy fat.

And puppy fat has a purpose. It shows that your body is changing, and it isn't all changing at the same rate. It may take as many as six years for your whole body to finish growing. That's a period when you may have a hard time getting used to your new body, which is shifting in so many different ways.

In that time of growth, kids gain between 50 and 60 pounds. You eat lots then. Parents sometimes say that their kids are eating them out of house and home. But that's part of growing up.

Then There's Fat Fat

Even though baby fat and puppy fat may be nothing to worry about, they should not be excuses for plain fat — and too much of it. There are charts that talk about kids' heights and weights. But they don't tell the whole story. If you feel fat, you may be fat.

Try pinching your skin with your thumb and forefinger below your shoulder blade. If you can grab an inch or more of fat, then you may be overweight. If you've got rolls and creases in your front, that's too much fat. If you've got more than one chin, that's more than you need.

Your doctor or school nurse is a good person to chek with, if you feel worried.

The Calorie Connection

A pound of body fat contains 3,500 Calories. Check page 25 for some information about what Calories are. If you eat 3,500 more Calories of food than you burn up, then you store a pound of extra fat. And if you use up 3,500 extra Calories of energy, then you use up a pound of stored fat.

That's most of what there is to the secret of gaining and losing fat. You can check the chart of foods on page 27 to get some idea of what 3,500 Calories of food is. It's quite a bit.

People usually don't get too fat all of a sudden. They gradually add a little bit of fat, a little bit more, and pretty soon, there's too much extra stored up. And while all this is going on, people have been developing two habits that make this problem a hard one.

The Eating Habit

Suppose you need about 2,400 Calories of food a day to have all the fuel you need and not gain any weight. And suppose you've gained too much weight, and you're faced with the problem of losing it.

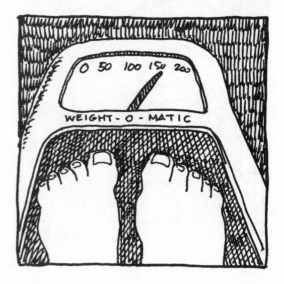

Eating less is a sure way to do that. If you cut back about 500 Calories every day, then at the end of a week, you'll have cut back 3,500 Calories and will have lost a pound.

That sounds easy. Well, it's an easier arithmetic problem than it is an eating problem. When you're used to eating a certain amount of food, food that you like to eat a lot, it's hard to just cut back. Talk to some people who have tried it. It's not such a snap, and for some people, it seems impossible.

People try all sorts of diets. They stop eating altogether for some time. They stop eating one particular kind of food, or they start eating a lot of another food. Sometimes these diets work, and sometimes they don't. Most often, magic kinds of diets don't last, and often they're not very healthy.

Eating habits are hard to change. Especially when you're surrounded with people who seem to burn up food so fast that they can eat and eat and eat and never gain a pound.

The Other Habit

How much energy you spend — that's the other habit. Studies have shown that among all the kids who are overweight, the main problem is not eating too much. In fact, many overweight kids don't eat as much as kids who don't weigh so much. The main problem has to do with how much exercise they get.

Kids just don't get as much exercise as kids used to. There's TV to watch, and kids sit and watch a lot of it. There are school buses, and there's the family car with parents to drive you when you've got to travel somewhere. For some kids this combination of things results in the problem of storing too much fat.

Nutritionists say that if overweight kids got an hour more of hard play or exercise every weekday and three hours on Saturdays and Sundays, there would be less of a weight problem today.

How many Calories you burn up exercising differs from person to person. Heavier people burn up more energy

doing the same things than lighter people. If it's very hot, you'll burn more Calories doing the same work than if it were cooler. And if it's very cold, your body burns more just trying to keep you warm. Here's an idea of how much energy you burn in an hour doing different things.

Getting Help

It's no fun to feel fat. It's worse when insensitive people call overweight kids fatso, porky, jelly-belly or tubby. Those names may sound funny to some people, but they hurt, and they're no help.

Being fat can make someone feel miserable, angry, all alone, and hopeless. If this is a problem for you, or for anyone you care about, it's important to talk to someone who can help. Even though making changes is up to you, a doctor or school nurse can help.

If an overweight problem isn't solved when you're a kid, it only gets harder when you grow up.

AN ENERGY CHART	
QUIET THINGS: WATCHING TV, EATING, READING, PLAYING CHECKERS	80-100 CALORIES PER HOUR
LIGHT ACTIVITIES: WALKING SLOWLY, PRACTICING A MUSICAL INSTRUMENT, DOING DISHES	110-160 CALORIES PER HOUR
MEDIUM THINGS: CLEANING UP YOUR ROOM (REALLY CLEANING IT!) WALKING PRETTY FAST, HOUSEHOLD CHORES	170-240 CALORIES PER HOUR
ACTIVE THINGS: BOWLING, EASY BIKE RIDING, PING-PONG	250-350 CALORIES PER HOUR

31
Another Big Problem: Malnutrition in the U.S.

American families do not eat well enough. That's what the U. S. Department of Agriculture learned from studying how people eat. They found that about 20 percent of American families eat poor diets. A poor diet means they're getting less than two-thirds of the recommended daily allowances of one or more nutrients.

Why? There are three reasons. Some people just do not have enough money to buy food in a big enough quantity or variety to supply what's needed.

A second reason is the largest one. Too many people eat too much food and the wrong kinds of food — too much sugar, starch, and fats. That causes overweight, which has become a national disease. Those foods give you energy but not much else. And they take up the room you need for other important foods in your diet.

What About Kids and Malnutrition?

What's wrong with the way kids eat? The U. S. Department of Agriculture has studied this too. And they've found some trends. They found that most kids get enough protein. Carbohydrates and fats seem to be no problem either. But here are danger spots — in three nutrients specifically: calcium, iron, and thiamin (that's one of the B vitamins). The foods that generally supply these nutrients are milk products and leafy green and yellow vegetables. How do you think you do in those two categories?

You may know some kids (maybe you're one) who seem to do fine on a diet of hot dogs, hamburgers, peanut butter, soda, and snacks. You may feel fine on such a diet. But you have no idea how you'd feel if you ate one that was more balanced. And many nutritionists feel that even though you are okay now, you're not doing the best for your grown-up body — the one you're growing now to live in for the rest of your life.

Missing food from one group isn't going to make you a nutritional failure, as long as it's not a regular habit. But why settle for less than best in anything? Especially when it's *your* body.

32
Will an Apple a Day
Keep the Doctor Away?

There are lots of different things that people have been saying about food for a long time. Here's a list of some of them.

1. An apple a day keeps the doctor away.
2. Fish is good brain food.
3. If you eat before you go to sleep, you'll have strange dreams.
4. You can't be healthy without eating red meat.
5. Chocolate causes acne.
6. Bread and potatoes are fattening.
7. Brown eggs are more nutritious than white eggs.
8. Carrots make your hair curly.
9. Beets make your blood rich.
10. Lemons make your blood thin.
11. Hard-cooked eggs are hard to digest.
12. Honey is less fattening than sugar.

Which of those do you think might actually be true? Which do you believe in?

Well, the truth of it is, none of them are true — not one. None of them have been scientifically proven in any way. And that's that.

What is true is that your body is very important and special. Your body deserves the absolute best you can do for it. That means you should learn to pay attention to what you feed it.

A Last Nibble

How do you know what's really right for you to eat? That's for you to decide. This book has given you a big chunk of information about food — where it comes from and what it does for you. But how you use this information is up to you.

Here's one more tidbit to think about. Food has a very special place in people's lives. Think about family gatherings, birthday parties, and other celebrations in your life. Food is an important ingredient in all those occasions. Then eating is part of a wonderful, joyful, sharing experience. That's important to remember: food is to enjoy too. Chew on that for a while.